Laws of the
JUNGLe

Dating For Women Over
40

Gloria MacDonald & Thelma Beam

Laws of the Jungle
Dating For Women Over 40

By Gloria MacDonald and Thelma Beam

ISBN: 978-0-9783360-0-4
Copyeditor: Christine Frank, www.christinefrank.com
Cover and Interior design: Toolbox Creative, www.toolboxcreative.com
Cartoons: Everyday People Cartoons (copyright) Cathy Thorne,
www.everydaypeoplecartoons.com.

Dedication

GLORIA

For Eric

THELMA

For Cricket

Acknowledgements

There are so many people to thank for their help with this book! First and foremost, Larry Beam and Eric Kay, our two sweethearts, who listened to many stories and theories and never failed to lend us a comforting shoulder. Gloria knows that "for me, the book wouldn't be, if it weren't for Eric's incredible patience, untiring support, and incredible pride in me. I can't thank you enough for putting up with two and a half years of late nights and long weekends at the computer. We've all heard of the golf widow, well, you were the book widower. I love you so much." Thanks to Andrew Kay, Gloria's teenaged stepson, a constant source of amusement and joy, who provided wonderful insights into how kids see their parents and dating. Thelma wishes to thank her husband Larry for his brilliant insights into the male psyche, his eternal faith in his wife, his steadfast support, and his unique mixture of pie-in-the-sky optimism and down-to-earth common sense.

Special thanks go to Jan King, who gave us the courage to "go for it" because of her professional opinion that we actually had a publishable book idea. She continued to guide us through the publishing jungle and gave us much good advice. We'd also like to thank Cathy Thorne, for her wonderful cartoons of Everyday People. Dawn Putney and her team at Toolbox Creative, for their creativity and resourcefulness in cover and interior design. Christine Frank, for her sharp eye and honed copy editing skills. Our public relations expert, Linda LeBourdais, for helping us get the book launched. Sharon Marks, an incredible friend, who helped with all sorts of things, as only great girlfriends do, from technology and website design, to brainstorming and marketing ideas.

Thanks to Hugh Oddie and David McNab for introducing us to one another in the original marketing research project we did together. Our Perfect Partners clients, and all the men and women who shared their intimate stories with us. Special thanks to Joan Kent, an incredible woman, from whom so much has been learned. Without Joan, Perfect Partners wouldn't run as seamlessly as it does. And thanks to Nicole Bourgeois, a very bright and talented woman, for helping with all of the behind-the-scenes details.

Finally, our long-suffering friends who gave us their untiring feedback on everything from titles, fonts, alternate versions, cover designs, and copy. Every woman needs those special girlfriends who are there for them through all the ups and downs. Gloria wouldn't be here today if it weren't for her two dearest friends Jule Zacher and Gaby Lowry, who have been there for her through divorce, dating (the good, the bad, and the ugly), tears, laughter, crazy ideas, you name it!

Thelma greatly appreciates the unstinting support and guidance given by her friends: Karen Poppell, who advised me to "keep it simple," Kathy Goggin for keeping me sane, Linda Lew, for giving me a reality check every once in a while, Marillene Allen who is unashamedly proud of my accomplishments, Heidi Von Palleske for her honesty, George Gillies for explaining the ways of the world, and Michelle Massie for her unrelenting optimism.

Contents

Introduction

Our Story
By Gloria and Thelma

We've been meeting for tea at the Four Seasons since some time in 2004. At first just because it was such a girly-girl thing to do; now we get together about once a month to work on our book. We always have the same hostess. She greets us warmly and calls us Ms. Beam and Ms. MacDonald. She knows what kind of tea we like and brings us extra clotted cream now, without our even asking!

As individuals, we probably couldn't be more different. By all of our own measures, tests, and theories, two people like us would *never* make a good match for a romantic relationship. In fact, we kind of laugh at ourselves and how different we are. As working partners, however, we create a great balance, and bring different strengths to the table.

Thelma is a practicing psychotherapist and the principal of Mind Meld Consulting Inc, a marketing think tank specializing in consumer motivations. She is the analytical and research brains of the team. All of the facts and statistics in the book, which prove our points, are thanks to her work. She's a logical thinker and a planner, and is very organized. She was really the one who pulled our ideas together in an intelligent, sensible order. Chaos and

Thelma are not one! Thelma is always on time for tea. If the truth were known, she's probably always early.

Gloria is a people person. She gets all of her energy from being around people and cares deeply about how they *feel*. She's interested in Thelma's facts and figures, but would never have the patience to actually dig them all up. Many of the real-life stories in the book, which demonstrate our theories, come from Gloria's experience with people. Gloria is highly spontaneous. If she didn't have some level of chaos in her life she'd probably be bored. Gloria is always trying to cram one more thing into her schedule, is always running late, and has never once in all of this time, despite her best efforts, arrived at tea before Thelma!

Thelma would probably never have started this book without Gloria. Gloria would *definitely* never have finished the book without Thelma.

Thelma met her husband when she was in college. She got married at the age of 20, and has been married to the same man for twenty-eight years.

Gloria also met her husband when she was in college—well, at least her first husband—and got married three weeks after she graduated, at the ripe old age of 22. Gloria was also married for a long time, almost eighteen years; it's just that it was to two different men, neither of whom she's married to any longer. Gloria is now in a third, wonderful relationship.

Thelma knows what it's like to have a successful relationship and to be married to one man, and have that sense of stability and structure.

Gloria understands firsthand just how tough it is to find yourself single again in the middle of your life. Not something any of us ever expect, or plan for.

Despite our very different personalities, experiences, and approaches to life, we both saw the same very interesting challenges and patterns evolving from our work with single professionals, 40 years old and over, who were looking for relationships.

It all started in 2003 when we met. Gloria was looking for some market research expertise in order to help her understand the key differences in marketing to single professional men versus women in the 40-plus age range. This is the target market group of prospective clients for her company, Perfect Partners. As the name suggests, Perfect Partners is a dating and introduction service, and Gloria is a professional matchmaker. Gloria got started in this business because of her own personal experience of finding herself single again in her mid-forties after a second divorce. After three years with only two dates, she realized it was really tough out there. Much to her surprise, she ended up using a dating service, but to no avail. She then realized there was a huge need for a very personalized service that caters to 40-plus professionals. She decided she was going to give it a whirl and launched Perfect Partners.

"What do people buy when they buy a dating service?"

That was the question we had originally set out to answer. In the course of many interviews with prospective clients, focus group discussions, and studying statistics of single men and women, we did answer this question for Perfect Partners. But it just raised more questions about the whole process of dating: What, indeed, do people get out of it?

Many of the women we interviewed had been in marriages which ended up in divorce, or were widowed, or had other long-term relationships which came to an end. They hadn't dated in many years and had no idea what to expect. There was a sense that things had changed from what they remembered, and not for the better! Meeting and keeping men was more difficult; men less plentiful; rules different. Sometimes they felt like dinosaurs. It could be scary. And dates could be truly horrible. We heard many, many bad date stories which would be hilarious if they weren't saying something so tragic. You know what we mean. The blind dates who seem to have been raised by wolves, those with no manners, the ones who couldn't make a decision if their lives depended on it, the men who talk constantly about their ex, the ones who are so boring you almost fall asleep between courses. And the heartbreakers. The good ones who were fun and witty, sexy and attentive. You spent the whole evening with them, and they swore they'd call, but they never did. Truly dreadful! Why would women put themselves through this?

In contrast, men approached dating in a very different manner than did women. Men who recently came onto the relationship market looked at the prospect of dating like kids in a candy shop. Wow! There were so many really nice, attractive women out there! Who knew? In fact, our most alpha of males was a 70-plus divorcé who dated often, and dated women that the other, younger men would have killed to take out themselves. And dates were generally fun and exciting. The women were great company. They could hardly wait to meet the next one. This is not to say that men never tire of dating, or that they don't have dating challenges. They do. But their point of view, outlook, and expectations are generally different from women's.

From all of our findings and experiences we saw a book evolving, specifically to help the millions of single women who are out there experiencing the brave new world of dating over 40. It's not like it was when we were in our twenties and there were lots of eligible young men everywhere! Life is different and the rules for dating, or as we call them, the "Laws of the Jungle," have changed. No, we're not in our twenties any longer and neither are the men with whom we're having relationships. We saw lots of women who were struggling to survive in this jungle, who were not at all sure how to navigate in this treacherous new territory.

We hope this book helps you understand how the Laws of the Jungle are different, why they are different, and how you can find your way to a new and wonderful relationship with a fantastic man. Why should you believe us?

Gloria MacDonald, through her matchmaking business, has introduced over 1200 couples and has interviewed hundreds and hundreds of single men and women. She's heard the stories, the good, the bad, and the ugly from both sides, men and women.

Thelma Beam is a psychotherapist in private practice. She specializes in helping men and women with relationship issues: those who want to be in relationships but aren't, those who are in unhappy relationships, and those recovering from relationship disasters. She is also the owner of Mind Meld Consulting Inc., a marketing think tank that uses established principles of psychology to understand consumer behavior.

Together, we knew that we had the right combination of skills and knowledge to help women over 40 find a wonderful man.

Is our book for you? Ask yourself the following questions:

1. Are you a woman who is 40-plus and single?

2. Have you recently come out of a long-term relationship or marriage, either through divorce, separation, or bereavement?

3. Do you think you might want to start dating again, but feel you might be a bit rusty?

4. Alternately, have you gone through a series of relationships over the years, but feel it's time to settle down for good now?

5. Do you wish to share your life with a wonderful man?

6. Do you feel out of place in bars and nightclubs?

7. Are you a successful professional who feels it's inappropriate to date colleagues or clients?

8. Do you know exactly the type of man you are looking for?

9. Have your friends been less than helpful in introducing you to potential dates?

10. Is your biological clock ticking? Do you think you might want to have children very soon?

11. Do you feel like men your age are usually looking for younger women?

12. Do you feel like there are just no good men out there?

If you answered "yes" to one or more of these questions, then *Laws of the Jungle: Dating For Women Over 40* is the book for you.

WHERE THE ☆⁈⁎ IS THAT PRINCE?

Chapter 1
The Laws of the Jungle

In our fairytale dreams, Prince Charming is supposed to ride up on his white horse and sweep us off our feet. Too bad this is real life. And for the first time in real-life history we have a whole generation of men and women who are finding themselves single in the middle of their lives. Astronomical divorce rates and the phenomenon of women postponing marriage because they've become more career-oriented and self-sufficient have changed our demographics. Face it, whether we like it or not, we're pioneers of middle-age singledom. We're blazing trails, cutting new paths, figuring this all out on our own. Our mothers can't help us. There are no tried-and-true rules that have been passed down through generations by those who have gone before us.

But if everything has changed, if it's a new world order out there in the vast abyss of dating, if it's all so difficult, if finding a man is so tough and relationships are so challenging, why don't we just give up? Well, because frankly, some things haven't changed. It doesn't matter how young or old we are, we're wired for companionship, a special intimate relationship with one person. And no matter what stage in life we're at when we find this wonderful relationship, we can still fall in love and feel just like we did when we were teenagers.

Both women and men are looking for relationships. We want to fall in love; we can't get away from it. It's instinctual. We all have basic emotional needs. We're looking for a mate who accepts us, wants us, and is committed to our well-being. We have found in our interviews with hundreds of single men and women who are 40 and over, that with few exceptions, men and women are both looking for the same thing: committed, monogamous relationships.

Here are some of the things people have said about why it is important for them to find a mate. Can you guess which were said by women and which were said by men?

1. "I find it rewarding; more fulfilling than being alone; sharing enjoyable experiences with someone; being able to please someone else, bring pleasure to someone else." *BT, Age 49*

2. "I like to share things. I like to nurture and be nurtured. It would be nice to have someone notice I'm not there. I want to be mutually supportive." *JR, Age 66*

3. "The companionship; I want to share the adventures with a person, be able to look back and say 'Remember when we did that?' I want a partnering – two people can do so much more together than separately." *SS, Age 41*

4. "Sharing things and partnership are important. At my age it's like having a garden to nurture. I want to share victories and triumphs with someone; grow together in knowledge and age. I'm looking for someone to make music together."
    RI, Age 49

5. "There's a little space there that's empty. It would be nice to share things with someone. I'm ready; it took a while. It would be my pleasure to be exceedingly good to someone and do special things for them. It would be great to have someone at the top of a ski hill to say 'Gee isn't this a trip?' I'd like to kiss someone on New Year's Eve. Having sex would be nice."   *KR, Age 55*

6. "I want to share my life; that's what I miss. When I open the paper and I'm reading something I want to be able to say 'Do you believe this?' Taking walks, playing tennis, sharing a meal—that's what I miss."   *YC, Age 51*

7. "Companionship, intimacy, I like being with someone, it's natural. I like married life and sharing. I would love to build a house that would reflect 'our' lifestyle."   *TM, Age 60*

8. "As human beings we're enhanced by a partner in a different way than a friend. We're made to be pair bonded. It's important for most people to have a partner. You could be sitting doing nothing, but you know they're there."
    TD, Age 48

9. "I want/need someone to share things with. I want to have a soulmate, someone you have no secrets from, someone with whom you can share the good and the bad, all the ups and downs. With the right person, everything feels good."
    JW, Age 51

10. "I've been by myself for a while. I'd like to find someone to share my life with, that's what's missing. I can flirt with anyone, but I have so much to offer another person. I've always pictured myself as having children. I'd like to increase my chances of meeting someone." *JS, Age 41*

11. "As a general rule, people are social animals. The world is made for couples. It's much more fun and pleasant to spend time with someone else. It's nice when you've had a bad day at the office to have someone to come home to."
CS, Age 54

12. "Life would be better – there's more out there that I don't experience. I want to have someone to share things with. But, it's better to be alone than in a bad relationship."
KM, Age 46

Quiz Answers: 1. male, 2. male, 3. female, 4. male, 5. female, 6. female, 7. male, 8. female, 9. male, 10. male, 11. female, 12. female

Over and over again, men and women say the same things. They're looking for companionship; someone to share their lives with; someone to share the joys and sorrows with; someone to come home to at the end of the day; someone to grow old with. Both men and women are looking for that special someone who they know will be there for them, that special person for whom they are the most important person in the world. Yet if we're all looking for the same thing, if we all have this innate instinct and need for intimate companionship, why does it seem so difficult to find?

Gloria's Personal Note

My parents had one of those seemingly rare, incredibly happy marriages. I only remember them fighting once in my life, and that was when I was twelve. They had a fight while hanging wallpaper in the dining room. After fifty years together they were still best friends, they held hands all of the time and kissed each other openly and often. I'm sure, like any couple, they had their challenges, but they weathered the storms and were genuinely happy and in love. Then, suddenly, my mom passed away and it was all over.

When I arrived in Houston at my folks' house the next morning, things were much worse than I had imagined. My parents had a very traditional marriage: my dad worked hard and supported the family financially, and my mom took care of the kids and the house. I knew my father didn't know how to cook. My father had had a cup of coffee every morning for the past fifty years. I wasn't surprised that he didn't know how to boil a pot of water, but I knew things were really bad when he didn't even know where the coffee was kept! I spent the next week helping my dad take care of things and teaching him how to run the washing machine and dryer. I took him to the grocery store to try to help him get a sense of what he could buy that would be easy to prepare. At one point I remember turning to my brother, who had also flown in from thousands of miles away, and saying "Dad's sure going to be surprised when he finds out these dishes don't automatically put themselves in the dishwasher!" Needless to say I was worried about how Dad was going to survive.

I underestimated him. My dad is a survivor. Just about a year after my mom died, the phone rang one night. It was Dad. He called to tell me that he had met someone. He had a girlfriend! He was so excited. He sounded years younger. You could tell he felt like he was 16 again.

. . . .

Can you imagine! If a man who is almost 80 years old and hasn't been out on a date for over fifty years can do this, surely we can too—if we choose to. My father had to learn about the new rules for dating. Things had changed just a wee little bit in the last fifty years. At times he would call me up and ask me how often he should be calling his girlfriend, or who should be paying for what. It was quite cute, and very wonderful. But things definitely had changed, and the rules were different. Even my father had to learn the new rules.

Okay, so now we've established three things:

1. It's a jungle out there. It's really tough to be a single female 40 and over trying to find a man.

2. No matter how tough it is, we can't help it. We, both women and men, are innately driven to find a mate.

3. And, as if it weren't difficult enough already, life has changed. It isn't what it used to be when we were in our twenties. The laws of the jungle are new and different.

As we worked with single women we could see how the laws of the jungle work in real life. We observed tactics that worked, and tactics that failed miserably with men. We saw that there are indeed some women who are easy to find men for, while others are very difficult. What is it that makes these women different? We asked ourselves how a woman over 40 can get the man she wants without having to sacrifice her soul or her dignity in order to do it. We've tried to help you by giving you answers to these questions.

This book is for the twenty million single women over 40 in North America who want to beat the odds and find the man of their dreams! Despite our dose of realism, we've written the book to help, encourage, and give you a better chance. This is a practical book that not only tells you what to do to increase your chances, but also tells you why you need to do it. The fact is it really is a jungle out there! There are lots of very real, valid reasons why it's extremely difficult for single women to find the man of their dreams—but NOT impossible. We've tried to set out for you the laws of survival in this jungle.

THE SEVEN ATTITUDES OF HIGHLY SUCCESSFUL DATERS

The thickest jungle you'll have to slash through in the world of dating is the jungle that exists in the six inches between your ears. The mental jungle. As with all things in life, your attitude, mindset, and the level of your desire to succeed will ultimately play a huge part in determining the outcome of your search. We find, when working with single women, that their mindset and attitudes play a big role in how successful they are in finding a partner. If they have a positive view of men and believe in their prospects of finding a partner, their chances of finding a mate are much higher than those women who have negative attitudes about men, and/or have little faith in their ability to ever find a suitable mate. After all, if men are such tiresome, lowly creatures, as many men-bashing jokes would have us believe, then why would you want to own one? And if you really don't believe that you have a chance of finding a good man, then why put yourself through the frustration of looking? These sorts of attitudes create ambivalence and trepidation. We have seen over and over again that women who have a positive attitude have a much easier time in the dating jungle than those who don't. What do we mean by "positive attitude"? Here is our list of the seven attitudes which are held by highly successful daters. In our experience, women who display these attitudes have a much better start on finding a partner than those who don't.

Attitude #1 – Belief in the Possibility

Henry Ford said "If you believe you can or you can't, you're right." Dating is no different. If you believe you will, or will not find a partner, you're right. The highly successful dater has a positive attitude about her ability to find and have a wonderful, loving relationship. We attract what we focus on and what we think about expands in our experience. So if you catch yourself saying or thinking any of the following, STOP. Reverse the thought.

"There are no good men left."

"I really don't think this will ever work."

"I'm no good at dating."

"I always seem to attract losers."

"My ex was such a jerk."

"I'll probably spend the rest of my life alone."

"I don't want to spend the rest of my life alone."

Attitude #2 – Open-mindedness

We all have things that we think we're looking for in a mate. You may even have made up a list of characteristics, personality traits, and shared interests which you feel are very important. Wouldn't it be lovely if finding a partner were as simple as walking up and down the aisles of a grocery store and pulling your choice off the shelf! Lists are all very well, but successful daters are willing to chuck the list and do some impulse buying if the product seems interesting. The most successful daters are those who are willing to remain open to meeting a variety of people, even if those people don't necessarily meet all the criteria they *think* they're looking for.

Attitude #3 – Suspending Judgment (The 3-Date Rule)

As human beings we can't help but make instant assessments of the people we meet. It's something our subconscious minds just do automatically. We can't turn that instant first impression instinct off. What we can do, however, is consciously decide that we're going to withhold judgment of the person we're meeting until after we get to know him or her a little better. All of us have had situations in life where our first impression of a person wasn't necessarily accurate, and not just in a dating situation. Don't limit yourself by cutting off your options because your first impression of someone didn't sweep you off your feet. We highly, *highly* recommend you live by the 3-Date Rule. Tell yourself you're going to suspend judgment on the person until you've been out with them at least three times. You'll be amazed at how far off base some of your first impressions may be.

Attitude #4 – Honoring

A commitment to honoring our fellow human beings is a key factor to the highly successful dater. The truly successful dater has a code of honor for dating. Just like with the military, or any successful team of people, a code of honor is critical to success. A code of honor puts mission first, team second, and the individual third. If your mission is to find a mate, your actions may need to follow a "Do whatever it takes" mentality to get the job done. This means honoring your mission enough to step out of your comfort zone; doing something new and different to meet that special person. The successful dater always puts team above individual, or themselves. This means honoring the other person, the person you're about to meet or have just met. You have a code of honor that you hold yourself to which enables you to honor the other person in the way you would want to be honored. This includes refusing to be critical, judgmental, or nasty. Even if you've just had what you think was the worst blind date of your life, you honor and appreciate the good in your "team" member. You're willing to see that we are each a wonder of uncharted territory in the universe. We will never fully know the depths and beauty of another person; in fact, we will never truly know ourselves completely. Lastly, you honor yourself. You don't rehash every second of the conversation and berate yourself for everything you said or did. You refuse to think of yourself as inadequate or undeserving. You hold yourself as a wonder of uncharted territory in the universe, and do not allow yourself to take "rejection" personally.

Attitude #5 – Enjoyment and Celebration

Highly successful daters don't take dating on as a huge, serious, grueling, arduous job. Instead, they have an attitude of enjoyment. She, a woman in this case, is as serious as can be about wanting to find a life partner, but she makes a conscious decision to enjoy the process of meeting new people. She is able to celebrate all of her dating successes. No matter how small the success is, even if it's just that she got a phone call from a man (but didn't meet him). Successful daters are even able to celebrate rejection, and perhaps laugh at their dating "failures." After all, every time you meet someone who isn't the right match for you, you're one step closer to finding the right one! Successful daters are always able to find something to enjoy and celebrate in the situation. Maybe it wasn't the most stimulating conversation you've ever had, but the food was excellent. This isn't an issue of Pollyanna-like optimism, but a matter of conditioning the brain for success. Professional athletes spend hours and hours on psychological coaching. They work at programming the brain for success. Smart daters do the same thing to condition themselves for success.

Attitude #6 – Patience

The highly successful dater is able to remain patient with the process, and understands that sometimes it really is a process. Once you've made the commitment to finding a mate, sometimes everything falls into place quickly and you soon meet Mr. Right. Other times there still might be some learning and growing that will help you along the way. The successful dater doesn't throw her hands in the air after she's met two or three people and say "This will just never work for me." The highly successful dater takes each experience as an opportunity for learning and remains open to ways in which she might continue to develop. She is willing to listen and take feedback in the spirit of constructive input. She is willing to think about what part she is playing and the level of success she's having as a dater, and to make changes where appropriate.

Attitude #7 – Acceptance

The ability to accept love whenever and however it's given is a critical factor for the highly successful dater. Highly successful daters see themselves as loving, lovable, and loved. They know that in order to be able to give love they have to be able to accept love. Love is a full-on, give-and-take sport. This means you are able to accept love in all forms, from all sources. You can accept a compliment from someone you don't know without embarrassment. You can accept an invitation for a date as recognition and acknowledgment of your own positive qualities, even if you can't, or don't, want to accept the invitation. You can accept the generosity of a total stranger on a "blind date" buying you a cup of coffee, no matter how inexpensive, as a sign that the other person is honoring you as a valuable human being. You can accept with grace that someone is attracted to you, even if you don't feel the same attraction. With this acceptance you can experience similar grace when the tables are turned and you are attracted to someone, but the attraction isn't returned. The highly successful dater actually experiences that all mankind is loving, lovable, and loved.

✆ LAW OF THE JUNGLE ✆

The dater who fully embraces these Seven Attitudes of Highly Successful Daters can't help but have a life full of rich, loving, and rewarding relationships, including a wonderful relationship with that incredibly special perfect partner.

The very first thing you have to do, then, is to open yourself up to the possibility that the right man is not only out there, but HE IS ALREADY YOURS. You just have to find him. Don't think of this as a chore, but as a quest.

Why Do You Want To Be In A Relationship?

Why do you want to be in a relationship? Why do you want to go through all the effort of trying to find a man? As with most things in life, the greater the *why*, the easier the *how*. Most of us wouldn't willingly walk across a plank between two buildings ten stories up in the air. But, let's say your three-year-old child is on the roof of one of those buildings, and that building is on fire. Your only chance of saving his life is to walk across that plank to get him. All of a sudden your fear of heights is insignificant compared to your need to save your child's life. The "why" you need to get across to the other building is so great that the "how" you're going to do it becomes easy.

So, you need to know *why* you're looking for a relationship. Why is this important to you?

EXERCISE

Write down at least ten reasons (the more the better) why you want a man in your life. Why do you want a relationship? What is it about having a relationship that's important to you? What do you like about being in a relationship? Be specific.

Now write down ten reasons why you like being single and on your own. Even if you really don't like being single, come up with ten possible reasons.

Now go back to each of your statements and score each reason on a scale of 1 to 10, with how important this is to you. A score of 1 is not important at all, and a score of 10 is extremely important. When you're scoring this, think about how you would feel if you spent the rest of your life alone without any significant relationships. Add up your score for the reasons why being in a relationship is important to you, and subtract your total score for the reasons why being single and on your own is important to you. If you're reading this book we're assuming that your score is going to be relatively high.

Hopefully this exercise has helped you put some things in perspective. Just how great is your "why"? Are you willing to spend the rest of your life alone? If so, then maybe it's not important enough to you to move out of your comfort zone. If, on the other hand, you know you absolutely do not want to spend the rest of your life alone, and/or you know you want to have children and you don't want to be a single parent, then your "how" should become somewhat easier. Not that it's necessarily going to be a piece of cake for you to do something new and different and move out of your comfort zone. But if finding a man is so important to you, then you know you *must* do this. You must go out and try new things. You're going to have to take initiative in areas where you probably never have before. You're going to have to do some things differently. Most importantly, you're probably going to have to make some mindset changes.

Don't worry; we're here to help you through this jungle. We want to give you the best possible chances of survival. We'll show you what you need to consider changing, why you need to think about this, and how you can do it.

Chapter 2
Relationship Economics

"Where are all the good men?"

"All the great men are taken."

"Are there any decent men left?"

"The good men get snapped up right away!"

Have you ever said these types of things? Have you heard a girlfriend making statements like these? Are they really true?

Here are some of the most maddening things we have heard women say when they can't seem to find a man, or have just come out of a relationship.

"I know I don't need a man to complete me."

"I need to have a loving relationship with myself."

"I don't need a man in my life in order to be happy."

Ever since the grandiose days of feminine idealism known as the Women's Liberation Movement, women in Western society have been given one or another version of "A woman needs a man like a fish needs a bicycle." Surely Gloria Steinem never imagined the havoc that this statement would wreak to a whole generation of women looking for self-fulfillment. Men, we were told, are superfluous. Not necessary. Why, they're just sperm donors. Anything they can do, women can do better by themselves. The implication is that if a woman can't get along without a man, there must be something wrong with her. She is weak, downtrodden, a wimp.

There is no question that women can be strong and independent. The last forty years have shown just how strong they can be. In many arenas, women have not only equaled men, but have surpassed them. But have we evolved to the point where we no longer need to be in intimate relationships with men?

Is there something wrong with women who have a strong desire for a man in order to feel happy and fulfilled?

We feel that a woman is whole and complete just as she is. But this does *not* mean that there is something wrong with wanting to share her life with a man.

WHY WE ALL WANT RELATIONSHIPS

In the thirteenth century, the Holy Roman Emperor Frederic II conducted a very strange experiment. Frederic wanted to discover what language children would speak spontaneously if they had no parent speaking to them and teaching them. A group of babies were gathered together and caretakers assigned. The babies had all of their physical needs taken care of; they were fed, changed, bathed, and so on, but the caretakers were ordered not to speak to the babies or make any sounds. And before any of the babies could speak a single word, they all died![1]

Scientists have come far in the last fifty years in explaining what happened to Frederic's experimental children. In the 1950's John Bowlby came out with his highly controversial Attachment Theory, which, stated basically, says that humans, like animals, have an instinct to bond. Not just because bonding gratifies our physical and emotional needs, but because bonding, in and of

· · · · · · · · · · · ·

1   Thomas Lewis, MD, Fari Amini, MD, and Richard Lannon, MD, *A General Theory Of Love*, Vintage Books, New York, 2000, Chapter 4.

itself, is a primary human need. Furthermore, this instinct is activated at birth. Bonding, attachment, love: these things are all innate for us. We don't need to learn to do them. They come naturally. And male-female relationships are just slightly below mother-baby relationships in terms of survival and happiness.

You see, we can't help it. We are born with one overpowering instinct: the instinct to form relationships. But it's not easy! In American society, marriages are supposed to be the stable form of male-female relationships, but all too frequently, they do not last.

According to SIPP (The Survey of Income and Program Participation), the leading source of marital information from the U.S. Census Bureau, the probability of divorce increases as we get older:

PROBABILITY OF DIVORCE BY AGE

Age	Men	Women
35	20%	26%
40	26%	32%
45	35%	39%
50	40%	39%
55	37%	34%

Source: SIPP (Survey of Income and Program Participation, US. Census Bureau)

That is, by the time a woman is 40, if she has been married, she has a one-in-three chance of getting divorced. At age 50, her chances of being divorced rise to four in ten. And yet, despite the inevitable pain and heartache that accompanies marital break-up, people seem astonishingly eager to repeat the experiment! By age 40, 22 percent of divorced women have remarried at least once. By age 50, 29 percent have tied the knot again.

PROBABILITY OF HAVING REMARRIED BY AGE

Age	Men	Women
35	11%	16%
40	17%	22%
45	25%	27%
50	30%	29%
55	30%	25%

Source: SIPP (Survey of Income and Program Participation, U.S. Census Bureau)

There is no guarantee. Yet, people are driven to form these intimate types of relationships, not because we necessarily think it's the best thing for us, but *because we must.*

Relationships serve a number of purposes. They are a survival strategy, not only for individuals but for the species as a whole. After infancy, relationships are a way for us to grow emotionally and mature. In adulthood, "It's not what you know, it's who you know" that will help you get what you want out of life: an education, a mate, a job.

Dr. M. Scott Peck, in his book *The Road Less Traveled,* says that falling in love "is a genetically determined instinctual component of mating behavior. In other words, the temporary collapse of ego boundaries that constitutes falling in love is a stereotypic response of human beings to a configuration of internal sexual drives and external sexual stimuli, which serves to increase the probability of sexual pairing and bonding so as to enhance the survival of the species."[2]

Relationships are the only way that we currently have for fulfilling our biological destiny. When we look for a mate, we try to make ourselves as attractive as possible. Not for *his* sake, but to increase *our* chances of getting noticed. We modify our behavior to be more caring, loving, domestic, mysterious, or whatever we

2   Peck, M. Scott, M.D. *The Road Less Traveled,* Simon & Schuster, New York, NY, 1978, pg. 90.

think he will like best. It's a jungle out there, and we are competing with other women for the men of our choice. *Our choice!* If we don't want to settle for someone we don't really care for, then we have to increase our chances of attracting the men we desire most.

If he is also on his own best behavior and we come together, then we may fall in love, and everything becomes possible. All of our complex mating behaviors, and even the surreal experience of falling in love, are pre-programmed within each human. We don't learn how to do this; it simply comes naturally to us. *And it doesn't go away with age.* The instinct to form a relationship with a man does not extinguish past a certain age. It is a powerful force that drives us to seek relationships well past our childbearing years.

So why are women being told that they don't need a man and shouldn't have a strong desire to be in a relationship with a man? Well, one reason might be that **there simply aren't enough men to go around.** Those women who aren't paired up shouldn't have to feel like failures. But they shouldn't have to give up without a fight either.

This book is about giving women over 40 who want to be in a relationship with a man a fighting chance.

Two Solitudes

The whole dating industry today is big business. Personalized matchmaking services are hot, especially for the increasing number of well-heeled professional singles who are 40 and over. Through our work in this area, we wondered what expectations men and women bring with them on their dates. We interviewed dozens of single men and women, alone and in focus groups; had them fill in questionnaires; talked to them before and after their dates. In the process, we discovered two very different attitudes about their dating experiences, which we called the *psychology of scarcity* and the *psychology of abundance*.

Among the women we interviewed, there were two prevalent and permeating "truths" about their relationship prospects:

1. There are not very many single and eligible men out there, far fewer than there were when they were twenty, and

2. Among the men they meet, there seem to be a lot of "losers."

In contrast, we heard a diametrically opposite view from men:

1. There are lots of single women out there to choose from, many of them younger, and

2. Many of them are attractive, interesting women.

How could this be? What makes single women so cynical and single men so optimistic? Could it be true that there is a scarcity of single men and an abundance of single women? Yikes! Where have all the good men gone? We set out to find the answers.

Eventually, it all comes down to the laws of supply and demand. These are the true Laws of the Jungle. Only now we're talking about people and not commodities.

THE STATS: READ 'EM AND WEEP!

The U.S. Census Board is a veritable gold mine of population statistics. You can find out what people are doing now (by age, gender, race, or whatever else you want), and compare that with what they were doing forty years ago. Those who are willing to take on the daunting task of sifting through tables and tables full of complicated population statistics will be rewarded with a cornucopia of knowledge about their fellow Americans that they didn't even know they wanted to know! Fortunately, we have done this for you, and all you have to do is bear with us for the next few pages while we lay out the facts. Here are the highlights.

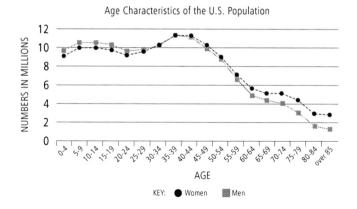

Age Characteristics of the U.S. Population

Overall, there are slightly more women in America than men, about 2 percent more. Initially however, more baby boys are born than baby girls. This is nature's way of compensating for a higher mortality rate among males. Males are bred to take more physical risks, and they are also more likely to go to war, which reduces their numbers later on. For the next twenty years or so, girls are a somewhat scarce commodity and boys must compete for them. Between the ages of 30 and 40, there are just about as many women as there are men, but thereafter, women begin to outnumber men. Not by much, not at first anyway. By age 49, women make up 51 percent of the population. At age 59, this increases to 52 percent, and by age 69, to 54 percent. It is only at age 80 and above that women seriously dominate the population.

Not too exciting, right? We then looked at marriage statistics for men and women and found something interesting: Women have pretty good odds to start with, but as they age, they become increasingly unlikely to be able to find enough men.

According to U.S. Census data (SIPP), women are actually a scarce commodity in their twenties and even into their thirties. At ages 25 to 29, there are approximately eight single women (never married, divorced, or widowed) for every ten single men, and at ages 30 through 34, there are still only nine single women for every ten single men. However, this abundance ends as women head into their forties. At ages 40 through 49, there is a shortfall of men for the first time, with the result that there are now only ten men for every twelve women. At ages 50 through 59, the shortfall rises so that there are ten men for every thirteen women. And at ages 60 through 69, it catapults so that there are ten men to every twenty-two women. The chart below shows the actual numbers of single men and women in the U.S. population at different ages.

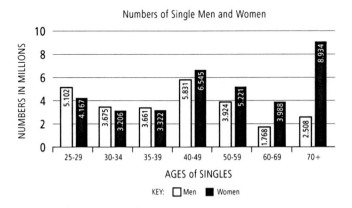

Numbers of Single Men and Women

You may well ask yourself: *What happened to the men? Why are there so many more single women than men? Shouldn't their numbers be roughly equal until after age 70?*

After all, there aren't that many more women than men in the population between 40 and 80. And this is where the really bad news comes in.

By age 40, most women have married at least once (90 percent), and slightly fewer men have married (86 percent). At any time, about 73 percent of each gender are still married. However, there are more divorced or widowed women in the 40-plus age group than there are divorced or widowed men. At age 40 through 49, we have 19 percent of women divorced or widowed compared to 13 percent of men. At ages 50 through 59, there are 25 percent of women divorced or widowed and only 19 percent of men. And at ages 60 through 69, 32 percent of women are divorced or widowed, while only 14 percent of men are in that category.

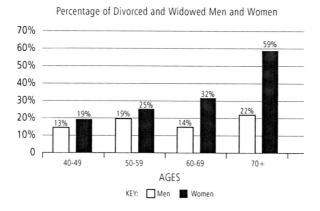

Percentage of Divorced and Widowed Men and Women

This data strongly implies that *men who come back on to the relationship market after divorce or bereavement are marrying. Unfortunately for you, though, they are marrying women who are younger than themselves.* What this means for women over 40 is that they must compete with younger women for the most desirable men. Or, put another way, they might need to *become* the younger woman! They might need to consider increasing the age range of acceptable men they'll meet and date.

⤜ LAW OF THE JUNGLE ⤛

If you want a fighting chance of being in a relationship, you may have to become the "younger woman." You may have to broaden your horizons and be willing to date a man who is five to ten-plus years older than you.

We added two additional filters to our estimates. The first filter removes ineligible singles from our calculations due to sexual orientation. Obviously, lesbian women are not competing for men, and gay men are not looking for women as partners. We estimate that approximately 15 percent of single men and 10 percent of single women are homosexual, and we removed them from the category of eligibility.

WHAT ABOUT THE LOSERS?

Finally, in response to our finding that many men are considered to be "losers," we included a "kooks and weirdos" filter in order to eliminate men and women who live on the edge and have addictions, compulsions, or eccentricities which make them largely undateable. We estimated that 10 percent of men and 5 percent of women might fall into this category.

Then, we proceeded to recalculate the number of single *and eligible* men and women in America, extrapolating from SIPP. This is what we got.

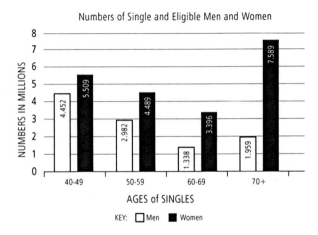

Numbers of Single and Eligible Men and Women

If you are 45 years old, your odds of meeting a single and eligible man in your age group are not great: there are ten men for every twelve women. For two of these women, there simply are no men their own age! If you are 55, there are ten men for every fifteen women in your age group. And if you are 65, there are ten men for twenty-five women. Those are terrible odds, especially when it seems that many men are choosing younger women. Too many of the men you meet are going home to a younger woman. You're not even on their radar.

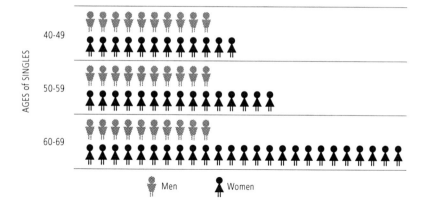

AGES of SINGLES

40-49

50-59

60-69

Men   Women

Now do you see the problem? There simply aren't enough single and eligible men to go around. Holy heartache! All those women we interviewed were right. And so were the men, the men who saw their prospects looking so bright.

There are some excellent theories as to how this all came about, but at the end of the day, all you need to know for the purposes of this book is that if you want to have a male partner that you love and desire, you're going to have to work for it, and possibly to change the way you approach dating and relationships.

Numbers do not lie. It is unlikely that any of the men and women we interviewed had ever calculated their relationship potential the way we did, by looking at census data. Even so, they understood their reality pretty well. The men knew exactly what kind of a sweet spot they were in. Men are supposed to be the "hunters," and are expected to "chase" women. And they do, early on, in their teens and twenties. But you can be sure that by the time they're in their fifties, there is very little in the way of chasing behavior going on, and quite a lot of cherry picking.

✎ LAW OF THE JUNGLE ✎

If you want a fighting chance of finding the man of your dreams forget playing hard to get! Honey, they ain't huntin' the way they used to any more.

I CAN NOT COMPETE WITH THE MAN
SHE WANTS ME TO BE.

Chapter 3

The Picky List

It's important to know what you're looking for in life. So let's start
with a very simple exercise, one you may have done before, but
humor us; do it again.

Exercise

Take three to five minutes to make a list of everything
you're looking for in a man. This should be a mind dump.
Don't spend hours contemplating this; just write and keep
writing. Write down everything that comes to you. Do you
have any specific physical requirements? Is the income
level of a potential partner important to you? What are

the qualities, characteristics, or personality traits you're looking for?

Now, go back through the list and put an "A" next to those things which you feel are "must-haves," those things that are truly a top priority for you. Put a "B" next to anything else. Hold on to this list. We'll come back to it later.

The one thing that's common among the potential dating service clients we meet is that they are looking to trade up, not down. Especially for those women coming out of divorce, they want someone who is better than their good-for-nothing creep of an ex-husband, not worse. We never hear a woman say "I'll take whoever you've got, I'm not fussy." By the time a woman is in her 40's or 50's, in many ways she is the best that she has ever been. She is sexually experienced, secure within herself, comfortable in her own skin. Years of working hard have paid off in financial security. Why should she settle for someone who is less evolved than herself?

This sense of entitlement usually translates into a list of specifications for a potential partner. When we interview women who join Perfect Partners, we find that many of them have specific criteria which, if not met, are an absolute deal-breaker for them. Some of these specifications are a direct result of their experience with a previous relationship: they want someone who is trustworthy, sincere, monogamous, and loyal. Sometimes the specifications are about their deep-seated emotional or spiritual needs: he must want children, or he has to be of a certain religion. Very often the specifications are about an anticipated lifestyle: someone who likes dogs, or someone who likes to travel or is a nonsmoker.

We listen to these criteria very carefully, because it seems to us that the clients are expressing their identity, who they are. You can't argue with these things. If a woman has been jilted by a faithless lover, she will not want to go through THAT again. If every fiber of her being is telling her that she needs to be a mother, and soon, that could well be the most important consideration in her life at the moment. And if she's been waiting her whole life to travel for romance and adventure, you're not going to talk her out of that.

"He has to like dogs."

"He has to want children."

"I want someone who is a Christian."

"Someone who lives within an hour drive."

"Someone honest and straightforward."

"He must be Jewish."

"Must like to travel."

"Must be a non-smoker."

We call these criteria "need-to-haves." It means you have a good understanding of the values and lifestyle that are important to you, the absence of which would make you incompatible with a man who does not share them. If religion is an important aspect of your life, then you want a partner who will understand this part of you. If you are an animal lover, and have a dog or cat that is part of your family, you won't be able to live with a dog-hater. If you don't drive and are afraid to fly, you don't want someone who lives far away or is a jetsetter. These things have to be respected, as they can make or break a budding relationship. In fact, we encourage you to sit down and make a SHORT list of the values or characteristics you wouldn't be able to live without in a potential partner.

However, we also encounter the Picky List. This is a list of superficial criteria that should NOT be on your list of deal-breakers.

"He has to have all his hair."

"I don't want anyone with a beard."

"He must be at least six feet tall."

"Someone who is fit and athletic."

"Teeth are really important to me. He has to have great teeth."

"No one who is more than three years younger or older than me."

"I want a doctor/lawyer/CEO of a large multinational company."

"Must make at least $150,000 a year."

And our personal favorite: "He has to look like THIS *(client holds up picture of her ex)."*

Here's what women don't seem to understand: every item you add to your Picky List carries a probability with it, a cost. There are only so many tall, good-looking, fit, and intelligent millionaires to go around. Believe it or not, we can't all meet a man who has everything, so we have to choose which criteria are most important to us and let the rest go. It makes us wonder if a woman really wants to find a partner when she's being so picky. Remember, it's all about the numbers and increasing your chances of success in the jungle.

Anne's Story

Anne is 57 years old. She has been divorced for thirty years. She was married for only a very brief time, and she hasn't had any terribly significant, long-term relationships since her divorce. Anne is very intelligent, highly educated, well-read, articulate, and cultured. She is spiritual, but not religious. She's keenly interested in astrology, theosophy, Buddhism, tai chi, and yoga. In addition to all of these interests, Anne is passionate about classical music, particularly opera. Anne insists on having only a man who shares her passion for opera and her interest in the spiritual. Anne has been going to the opera for thirty years on her own, or with a girlfriend. If Anne met a wonderful man who didn't like opera, couldn't she still keep going to the opera, just like she's been doing for the past thirty years? We don't know many women like Anne, let alone men.

. . . .

What's on your Picky List? Here are some of the most popular items we come across.

Height. It's unbelievable how many women, some of them small and petite, feel they can't do without a man who is at least six feet tall. Here's an idea of what it costs, in relationship terms, to date only men who are tall. As you can see in the chart below, the probability that an American man will be six feet tall or taller is about 14 percent. That means that you have automatically eliminated 86 percent of the men in your universe from consideration, making it much less likely that you will be able to find someone with all the other characteristics you are looking for.

AS TALL OR TALLER THAN…	PROBABILITY
6'0"	14%
6'1"	9%
6'2"	4%
6'3"	1%

Source: www.tallpages.com

So if you really think your ideal man HAS to be at least six feet tall, just be aware that you've made your hunt for Mr. Right a whole lot tougher. The taller the man has to be for you, the fewer men who will qualify.

At Perfect Partners, we can't help wondering just where on earth this magic six-feet-tall number comes from. There are so many women who say, "I'm attracted to tall men. I only want to meet a man who is six-feet tall or over. All the men I've ever dated have been six-feet tall or more." Wow, is that so? Honey, you better go right out and buy yourself a lottery ticket, because you are one lucky woman to have found so many men over six-feet tall! This must be the female equivalent of the man's fish story. "Wow! You should have seen that bass I caught last year. It was at least seventy-five pounds and forty-five inches long." Or, the man's longest drive, "I hit the best drive of my life on the sixteenth hole.

It went 310 yards straight down the middle of the fairway!" Not really! Maybe we *think* the man we're with is six-feet tall, because he feels like it to us. And the bigger he is, the smaller, more feminine, and better we feel.

Jane's Story

Jane's husband had very suddenly passed away the previous year. This woman spoke of her deceased husband as if all had been wedded bliss. Jane is five-foot three and weighs 110 pounds soaking wet. She's teeny-tiny petite. Well, guess what her magic number was. She was looking for a man who is at least six-feet tall...because her husband was!

Jane had been doing some online dating to get herself back in the game. She had many horror stories about the men she had met and what creeps and jerks they were. They certainly weren't the caliber of man she was looking for. That's why she decided to use a matchmaker. She knew that the quality of man she needed wasn't online. Jane had been used to a very nice lifestyle, and although she's only 51, she's fortunate enough that she really doesn't have to work. She does some part-time work so she can have extra money to travel and play with. Jane had a very long Picky List. Nevertheless, the first man to whom she was introduced met all of her criteria, which was truly a miracle. Doug is a very successful CFO of a significant company, active, fit, good-looking, right lifestyle, lots of similar interests, with kids who are grown and out of the house. Everything was great EXCEPT for one little thing: he's only five-foot ten. Jane was very reluctant to meet this man, ALL because he's only five-foot ten!

. . . .

Do we have to remind you again that it's a jungle out there?

Another criterion that women often set is that the man has to have a full head of hair. This would be the same as a man who demands that a woman in her fifties be a natural blonde. It COULD happen, but it's not very likely. Less than half the men in their forties have a full head of hair, and the situation worsens as they age. By the time they are in their sixties, only 35 percent have a full head of hair.

AGE	PERCENTAGE WITH HAIR LOSS
40-49	45%
50-59	55%
60-69	65%

Source: www.iwanthair.com

Another popular criterion is that the man must be slim and fit. But look at the statistics. By the time a man is between 35 and 44 years of age, there is already a 71 percent chance that he will be overweight. At ages 45 to 54, that probability increases to 76 percent. Which leaves only 24 percent of the men who are fit and slim. You have to ask yourself if it's worth eliminating three-quarters of the single male population in order to find someone who is slim and fit. Our advice is to learn to accept that beauty is only skin deep. It's not worth looking for a body builder if it means eliminating three-quarters of all the single and eligible men from your consideration.

AGE	PERCENT WHO ARE OVERWEIGHT
35-44	71%
45-54	76%
55-64	75%
65-74	76%
75 or older	67%

Source: U.S. Census – Health 2004

Susan's Story

Susan is a 46-year-old single mom with one teenager. She's been on her own for twelve years. Susan has a solid, successful career and a lovely home for which she's worked very hard. Susan is five-foot eight but with heels she's close to five-foot eleven. She's large-boned, could afford to lose a few pounds, and needs an updated hairstyle. Susan will **only** date a man who is between 46 and 49 years old, has a full head of hair, and is six-feet tall or taller, because she wants to feel feminine in high heels. Is there really a difference between a man who is 49 and 50? If Susan were 41 years old would she only want to date a man who was between 41 and 44 years old, or does she just have something in her head about that magic five-o number? How many men over the age of 46, 47, 48 still have all of their hair (see above)? If the man she meets has a full head of hair at 48, but starts to lose it at 50, will she fall out of love with him and leave him? And if she met a really wonderful man, who loved her and her child, had all the right qualities she's looking for, but was only five-foot eleven, couldn't she either wear flat shoes, or be slightly taller than him in heels? Does Susan already have the relationship she *really* wants? Maybe no close, personal, intimate relationship with a man at all?

. . . .

Finally, we find that about nine out of ten women we interview mention income as a criterion, whereas men rarely do. Usually, a woman sets this criterion because she does not want to have to support a man. Supporting a man financially has many negative cultural implications, and in pragmatic terms, she may just not be able to afford to do that. However, other women feel entitled to a high-wage earner. Some are looking to replace their ex-husbands; others are looking to upgrade their lifestyle. Whatever the reason, it should come as no surprise that high-wage earners are the exception rather than the rule.

Even a moderate income of $50,000 or more is achieved by only 38 percent of the men aged 45 to 54, in their prime wage-earning years. If a woman demands that a man is making a six-figure salary, she eliminates at least 90 percent of the men from consideration.

		MEN AGED	
	45-54	55-64	65+
$50,000+	38%	30%	7%
$60,000+	28%	23%	5%
$70,000+	21%	18%	4%
$80,000+	16%	14%	3%
$90,000+	12%	11%	3%
$100,000+	10%	9%	2%

INCOME

Source: U.S. Census Bureau

And it's not just about wages, either. During their forties and fifties, the prime divorce years, many men are financially wiped out by divorce settlements, especially if they have children. They may go from a sprawling four-bedroom house in the suburbs to a cosy one-bedroom apartment in town, which is all they can afford after the monthly payments on the house which their wife got in the settlement. But this does NOT mean that you should date only never-married men. As any relationship book will tell you, divorced men often make excellent husbands the second time around. They are already used to being married and many have learned from their mistakes with the first wife.

Dan's Story

Dan is 48 years old. He was married for seventeen years and has a 15-year-old daughter. Dan and his wife and daughter lived in a 4200-square-foot home in the suburbs with a large pool and hot tub in the back yard, a sauna and pool room in the basement, and lots of other amenities. When Dan and his wife mutually decided to go their separate ways, Dan moved into a 1200-square-foot condominium downtown and left his wife and daughter in their lovely suburban home. In order to do this, Dan had to cash in every dime of his retirement savings to be able to put a down payment on the condo and furnish it in a modest manner. Dan is a successful lawyer who makes a decent income, but is by no means rich. Dan's wife never went back to work after their daughter was born, so Dan is now paying a very significant sum each month in both child and spousal support. He never complains about this. He knows what the laws are, and this is simply what he's required to do by law. The fact of the matter is that Dan was on track to have his house paid off by the time he was 50 and be able to retire by the time he was 60 or so. Now that Dan is supporting two households, he doesn't have any retirement savings, he's slowly paying off back taxes, and he certainly doesn't have the disposable income he used to.

Dan is a loving, responsible man who has a very amicable relationship with his ex-wife and a very close relationship with his daughter. But Dan wouldn't cut the mustard for some women's financial expectations. Ask yourself who you're cutting out when you set your financial benchmarks for the elusive man of your dreams.

. . . .

Our advice is to remember that money doesn't buy happiness. As long as you have enough money to maintain a decent lifestyle between the two of you, then you shouldn't eliminate him from your list. What's really far more important to the ongoing happiness of your relationship is that the two of you have similar attitudes and outlooks on money. If one of you is a big saver and the other is a big spender, this is going to cause constant friction on a day-to-day basis throughout your relationship. We'll talk much more about this in Chapter 11 during our discussion on compatibility.

Exercise

Now, go back and review your list. Are there any "picky" items that have made it on your "A" list? Are there any items that maybe, just maybe, could be moved to your "B" list?

You have to remember that the more items you add to your Picky List, the lower the probability that you will meet someone with that combination of characteristics. Other women are also looking for a man who is tall, dark, handsome, and rich, but, as we have seen from the statistics above, these types of men are not as plentiful as one might wish.

∽ LAW OF THE JUNGLE ∽

Every item you add to your Picky List cuts your chances of finding that truly wonderful man; it doesn't increase them.

The Picky List and Sabotage of Love

How does it happen that some women get it into their heads that they deserve to marry an impossibly perfect man? Are these modern-day Cinderellas waiting for Prince Charming because of some misguided advice given to them by their mothers, or is there something deeper going on?

Women who want to be in a relationship find that they are constantly *adjusting* their criteria. It is an old adage that the things that attracted you to a partner in the first place are exactly the things which you will come to hate most after a time. For instance, if you married him because of his charm and easy way with women, you may come to hate that charm when you find him flirting with your friends or the young divorcée next door. Or, if you were attracted to him because he was so ambitious, you may get tired of sitting at home alone night after night while he concentrates on his career. Women learn from these mistakes and adjust their criteria accordingly. Probably the man you dreamed about as a teenager isn't the type of man you would be interested in today. Or maybe you are more realistic and realize that rock stars, football players, and movie celebrities just aren't your thing anymore. Most women find that they can fall in love with an imperfect being.

However, some women never do adjust their criteria. They keep the impossibly high standards of their girlish dreams and wait for Prince Charming to come along. In fact, they *deserve* Prince Charming, and no other man will do. This strong sense of entitlement can have two possible outcomes for them:

A) They can wait for exactly the right man to come into their lives, knowing that when they finally find him, he will fulfill every wish they ever had, or, more realistically,

B) They can wait and wait a long time, and the perfect man will never come.

They roll the dice and hope for outcome A above. What is important to understand though, is that EITHER outcome A or B is acceptable to these women. If they hit the jackpot, then fine. But if they don't, that also serves an emotional need—for sabotage.

Very often, what they say they need and what they do are diametrically opposed. They set these stringent criteria, not so they will be sure to get the man they deserve, but so they WON'T. They sabotage their chances for love even before they meet a man. That's how great their fear is. The more items on the Picky List, the greater the need for sabotage.

⤲ LAW OF THE JUNGLE ⤲
You can tell that you are setting out to sabotage yourself if no man seems to be good enough for you.

Very often, this sabotage of love comes in the form of an enormous ego. Women say that they deserve a man who is perfect (according to their own criteria), and that no other type of man will do. You would think that these women must be supermodels or brain surgeons, or have some other highly prized characteristics, but usually they are average women with average lives.

We are always baffled by a woman who has such stringent requirements AND expresses a desperation to be in a relationship. One such client is Evelyne.

Evelyne's Story

Early on in Perfect Partners history, we encountered a 31-year-old woman who lived in a small but nice one-bedroom apartment. Evelyne had a college degree and made $75,000 a year as a salesperson. Not a bad income. When asked if the income level of a potential partner was important to her there was no way to anticipate the answer we got. "Oh yes," she said. He had to make at least $450,000 per year because she wanted to live in one of two very posh neighborhoods in town, and she also needed to have a cottage on a lake that's well known for the lifestyles of the rich and famous. She was going to have at least two children and of course wouldn't be working after she had the kids, even though she would have a full-time live-in nanny. She wanted her children to go to very expensive private schools, and naturally they would be going to a very exclusive summer camp every year. She didn't care what the man was like on the inside; she was only looking for what he could give her. This was the saddest, neediest person we ever met!

. . . .

Evelyne's expectations were more than unrealistic, they were absurd. And yet, she listed them off with a straight face. Obviously she had spent a lot of time thinking about what she wanted and calculating her future husband's income. She had her whole life planned out, except for one small but pivotal problem: Men like this are very rare and would not generally be interested in a woman like Evelyne, who was very average. She had set her standards so high that failure was inevitable. At some level, she must have known that.

✸ LAW OF THE JUNGLE ✸

If you want a fighting chance of finding a man, (this one is thanks to Mick Jagger and Keith Richards) remember

You can't always get what you want,
If you try sometime,
You'll find,
You get what you need.

Chapter 4
Six Categories of Women

If nothing else, the previous two chapters of this book should have made you realize that relationships are essentially about survival of the fittest. If you're going to survive, you have to be realistic about your situation and develop strategies that will give you a better chance. So the first step is Self-Assessment. It's time for some introspection and honesty.

Six Categories of Women

Single females fall into fairly distinct categories. Which one of these comes closest to where you find yourself? Or maybe you see parts of yourself in two of these groups?

THE TICKING CLOCK GROUP

THERE ARE TIMES WHEN I SWEAR I CAN ACTUALLY
HEAR THE TICKING.

*"Currently, one out of every five women worldwide is delay-
ing having her first baby until the age of 35, a number that is rising
steadily..."* [3]

This group of women is in their late thirties to early forties.
Overall, most have never been married, and still want to have children. Many of them are very dynamic, accomplished women. They
have focused on their careers, and now they are ready to focus on
starting a family. Perhaps things haven't moved quite so smoothly
along the timeline they had originally envisioned when it really
came down to finding a mate, and now they are *desperate* to start a
family. Or at least they *say* they are. Their biological clocks are ticking

3   Source: www.sideroad.com

and time is of the essence. They don't have time to waste anymore, so they want to be married and pregnant within a year and a half. The challenge with introducing this group of women to potential partners is that men are not nearly as limited with respect to fertility as women are. Men can father children well after the time when it's seen as socially respectable. And in any case, they can always choose a younger woman to be the mother of their child.

As one man expressed it: "Bad planning on their part does not make for an emergency on my part."

For this reason, this group of women seems to have the biggest challenge in dating and finding that special man. Unfortunately, men who are 40 and over and still want children don't want to meet a woman who is over 38. Men seem to have this all worked out in their heads. They know that if they meet a woman who is 38, it will take them a year to get to know one another and get married. Now she's 39. They'll then only have one year to spend together and try to get pregnant before she reaches that ominous 40 number. Men just seem to KNOW that once a woman hits 40 it gets really tough to get pregnant and have children. They know that their chances of becoming a father with a woman 40 and over are significantly lower. Therefore, the smart wannabe father won't even meet a woman who is over 38!

To top it all off, these women are often unrealistic in their expectations and inflexible in their "requirements" for the man of their dreams. After all, they spent many years going to school and nurturing successful careers. They want a man who looks equally good on paper.

Men can just feel the pressure exerted by a Ticking Clock woman! Many men who would still possibly be open to having children, or more children, if they really met the right woman, are completely scared off by the urgency of this group. Most men can't guarantee that they absolutely will have children, and they feel this group of women is looking for a guarantee. Many men say it just wouldn't be fair to the women for them to even begin a relationship because they know how important the desire to have children is. Because men don't have the same biological age limitation on when they can father children, they have much more freedom, and for the most part, don't feel pressured into making a decision about whether they want to have children, or more children. Time is not necessarily of the essence to them.

Women in the Ticking Clock group, on the other hand, have a way of, if not exactly blatantly asking a man to commit on the very first date to having children with them, at least making their intentions very clearly known. This tends to send all but the very bravest of the male species running at breakneck speed in the opposite direction! They know it's not them who is important, but their sperm.

∞ LAW OF THE JUNGLE ∞

If you want a fighting chance of finding the future father of your children, don't even think of bringing up the subject the first time you have coffee together.

Our Analysis

At first glance, this group of women seems hard to sympathize with. How exactly did they manage to miss the gravy train in their high school or college years? Were they wasting time on math and medieval literature instead of investing it at the Friday night pub where they could meet other singles like themselves? Barbara Dafoe Whitehead, in her excellent book *Why There Are No Good Men Left*,[4] puts forward a very convincing theory of how women

---

4 Whitehead, Barbara Dafoe, *Why There Are No Good Men Left*, Broadway Books, New York, 2003.

have shot themselves in the foot in the post-Women's Liberation years. According to Ms. Whitehead, women today are operating on a different relationship paradigm than their mothers. In the past, young men and women were brought together in college or high school for the purpose of courting and mating. A girl could expect to meet her future husband in school, date him, and be engaged by the time they both graduated. If a career was in the cards for her, it was secondary to marriage. Now, that order has been reversed. When a girl graduates from college, she is prepared for a career, but not for marriage. She may have dated a number of young men, but does not plan or wish to marry until after she is established in a career. But by then, these successful, overachieving career women will encounter a man shortage, as they find that men who wished to be married have already found women who did not defer marriage for career. They find, in other words, that "there are no good men left" by the time they are ready to have it all.

Unfortunately, by the time a woman has achieved so much and is ready to settle down, her biological clock is *winding* down, and she finds herself on a critical path with timelines that are very tight. At the same time, she is out of practice with serious relationships and must learn a new skill set before she can achieve her goal. For the first time in her life, she is faced with the possibility that she may not be able to achieve everything she set out to do, that the world has stopped cooperating. If she is at all ambivalent about her goal of marriage and children, she will find a way to sabotage herself until it is too late.

Other women did not defer marriage and children on purpose. They just never found Mr. Right. And as their next birthday looms, they realize that it's now or never. What should they do?

Whether you've postponed marriage and children in order to establish yourself in a career or you just never found "The One," our advice is the same. If you are in the Ticking Clock group, you have an important and heart-wrenching decision to make:

Which is more important to you, the man or the baby?

This does NOT mean you cannot ever have both. It DOES mean that you MAY NOT be able to have both, at least not now, and you'll have to choose. You probably don't like the sound of this. You WANT BOTH and why should you have to give up what so many other women take for granted? We hate to repeat that this is the real world, a world that is ruled by the laws of the jungle. And in order to increase your chances of getting what you want, you may have to give something up first.

So close your eyes and picture yourself in a relationship with a good man (but no child). Imagine your home, eating dinner together, sleeping side by side, talking and cuddling. Good. Now, open your eyes. How did that feel?

Next, close your eyes again, and picture yourself with a baby in your arms (but no man). Feel her little body against you, imagine yourself feeding her, changing her, listening to her first words. Okay, open your eyes. How did that feel?

Now choose.

If you choose the relationship, it doesn't mean you won't have a child. But you *may* not, and that would have to be okay. Once the pressure is off to have a baby by a certain birthday, your chances of finding a great man increase tremendously. And there's also the option of adoption.

If you choose the baby, then **seriously consider becoming a single parent**. Talk to sperm banks, ask someone to be a donor, explore whatever possibilities are available for getting pregnant. It doesn't mean that you will never have a relationship, but you *may* not, and it won't be soon, and that would have to be okay.

Whichever you choose, go for it. The odds of finding a man *or* becoming a mother are much better than having to do both.

❦ LAW OF THE JUNGLE ❦

It's a paradox. Sometimes, in order to get what you really want, you have to give something up.

The Single Moms Group

This group of women is typically in their early- to mid-forties with young children (fourteen and under) at home. They are often working full-time and have primary custody of their children. The ex-husband takes the kids every other weekend, but otherwise, they are largely her responsibility. And a big responsibility it is!

James' Story

James, a 48-year-old man who was divorced with no children, ended a relationship with a woman he'd been dating for over six months. She was in her early forties, had been separated for about two years, and had two young children between the ages of five and nine. The woman was incredibly busy with her children's hectic schedules, driving them to and from piano lessons; dance classes; soccer, softball, and hockey practices; and games after school and on weekends. She also had a part-time job and was going back to school during the evenings. The children's father was involved in the kids' lives in a healthy way and was at the home of the ex-wife on a fairly regular basis for pick-ups and drop-offs, etc. James wanted to know: *"How are you relevant in a situation where there are young kids and the dad is still involved?"*

. . . .

Indeed, the smart man knows that these women are stretched to the max and only have time for a man in their lives every other weekend and one night a week when their children are with their father. This creates a whole other set of challenges. A man who is considering dating a woman in this situation is not only concerned about how much time and attention the woman will have to devote to him, he's also concerned about the relationship both the woman and her children have with the biological father. Many men are reluctant to take on the responsibility for someone else's children, especially if their own are already grown. Some men are concerned about blending families, if their own children are still young enough to be with them on a regular basis.

A single mom recently said that someone she'd been dating complained that "For you, your kids are always first, your career is second, and I'm third! There's not enough room in your life for everything. I don't see that changing." She agreed that it wasn't going to change, and the relationship eventually fell apart.

Natalie's Story

Natalie is a woman in her mid-forties who has three kids, aged 9, 13, and 15 years old. The children's father lives thousands of miles away in another country. The kids see their dad for three weeks during the summer. Natalie is obviously the sole caregiver for her children. She says she really wants to meet someone. She needs an adult relationship in her life and she misses having that special someone to share things with. When Natalie thought about how she would manage a relationship, she said she would probably be able to see a man on a Friday night about twice a month. She didn't think she'd ever be able to get away for a weekend. With her kids' schedules and all of their activities, she couldn't see how she would ever be able to leave her kids with her parents, her brother, or friends for a couple of days. She didn't think that would be possible. Now ask yourself, is it realistic to expect to be able to build a relationship with a man based on seeing him for a couple of hours twenty-four times a year? Most men would be looking for a whole lot more than that. Is Natalie ready to begin dating if she can't see her way to make more room in her life for a relationship?

. . . .

⚜ LAW OF THE JUNGLE ⚜

If you want a fighting chance of finding a man when you've got young kids at home, you're going to have to make room in your life for him, mentally, emotionally, and physically—or just forget about it until the kids are grown.

Our Analysis

The Brady Bunch were a blended family. Bob and Carol had three children apiece, and somehow they managed to date, marry, and raise all six kids with just the mildest sort of problems. So surely it must be possible, right?

The Single Moms group is faced with the very difficult, real-life challenge of how to balance everything in their lives: kids, careers, and dating. You may think that it's just a matter of efficiency—making the time for everything, but it's not that simple.

The great child psychologist D. W. Winnicott once said that there is no such thing as a baby without the mother. This means that mothers of small children can never be viewed as separate entities, but only as part of a symbiotic group. A mother and her children can be said to live within a family culture. Every family has one, and it's the parents who determine what is normal, what is valued, what roles each member will take, and so on. This is the way that children survive, become socialized, learn what is acceptable, and form an identity for themselves. When a new person is introduced into the family culture, there is always the potential for a culture clash. If the man Mom is dating happens to fit well into the family culture and is searching for a family, AND if his role doesn't violate someone else's *raison d'être* (ie, If the natural father is absent), then he can be incorporated into family outings, dinner, and watching TV. He can be turned into a chauffeur to take the kids to soccer practice or piano lessons, or even into a temporary babysitter while Mom is out food shopping. He becomes, in other words, a member of the family and begins to integrate into the culture.

However, if the man Mom is dating has his own family culture and is not looking for a new one, is just interested in pulling Mom out of her family and into his, or if the kids' natural father is present and involved, then the probability of integration becomes remote. He is not only irrelevant to the family; he has the potential to actually disrupt it. All the defenses of the family will then be mobilized to resist the invasion, oust the intruder, and bring Mom back into the fold.

If you are a Single Mom, you are faced with a really tough situation. You should know that, realistically, it's going to be very difficult to find a man who will understand that your kids always come first. Ask yourself truthfully whether a relationship is the right thing for you at this time.

If you decide that you still want a relationship and are willing to work hard and make compromises in order to get one, then you can increase your chances by choosing men who are most likely to fit into your existing family culture. Obviously, you must choose a man who likes children and doing family things rather than a man who wants to keep you all to himself.

Needless to say, if the children's father is still enjoying the benefits of your family dinners and family outings without the inconvenience of living with you, it is time to cut the cord. You must begin to live a separate life in order to create space for a new man.

❧ LAW OF THE JUNGLE ❧

If you don't think your life is crazy enough as a single mother, now you're going to have to become even more of an Olympic gymnast. We hope you're the master of flexibility and can do back bends, hand stands, cartwheels, and triple flips all while single-handedly preparing a three course meal for eight! (Well, maybe a touch of exaggeration.)

The Footloose and Fancy Free Group

Women who are 45 to 57 or so, are financially independent, and either don't have children, or have children who are grown and out of the house, are the Footloose and Fancy Free group. In many ways, this can be the easiest group of women to work with, *IF* these women are attractive and in good shape. If they are willing to meet men that are five to ten years older than they are, they are especially easy to match.

Women in this group are often quite independent. Many of them have been through the single-motherhood years. They may have spent the past eight to ten years of their lives "man-free," devoting their time and efforts to raising children and getting their feet back on the ground. Often they've gone back to school to get a graduate or post-graduate degree. They generally have a fulfilling career that they enjoy, but they're no longer putting in the twelve- and fourteen-hour days as slaves to their jobs. These women usually have a close group of female friends. They tend to love to travel. Their lives are busy, active and full—great really! EXCEPT they are just missing that one thing: a wonderful man to share their lives with.

There are a surprising number of women in this group who have no desire to get married, and often don't even want to live full-time with a man. Often these women like their freedom and independence; they like their "own space." They're looking for a permanent, committed, monogamous relationship. However, they want to spend three or four nights a week with a man and then be able to ship him off to his house for a couple of days.

Men in this same age range are generally in a very similar position of having financial stability, and having good, but not overly demanding, careers. They are usually looking for women who have time, energy, and the desire to enjoy life with them.

Our Analysis

You've probably heard it said that a woman is like fine wine: they get better as they age. And surely this time of life is a woman's golden age. They are mostly free from childrearing duties, have their careers well in hand, and are getting ready for the next phase of their lives, which might include a wonderful relationship with a great man.

Footloose and Fancy Free women do find themselves in a good life situation. Now it's just a matter of taking full advantage of it and cleaning up a few details. For instance, physical details relating to health and attractiveness; emotional details relating to men and relationships; and financial details relating to resources available to use in finding a special man.

If you are a woman in the Footloose and Fancy Free group, you are in a great place, but you're also the most likely to be competing with younger women for the best men. Men are much more visual than women, which means you have to feel your best and create the most youthful impression possible. We see you shaking your head. Why is it that men in your age group don't necessarily look *their* best but still expect to have an attractive woman on their arm? It's not fair! But it's the law of the jungle.

The biggest challenge for women in this age range is to stay youthful, attractive, and in good physical shape. If you are in the Footloose and Fancy Free Group, then you can get ready to find your perfect mate by:

- Joining a gym
- Getting a wardrobe and make-up makeover
- Eating sensibly or going on a diet
- Taking care of any minor medical problems that may exist
- Setting aside a "dating budget."

⚮ LAW OF THE JUNGLE ⚮

If you want a fighting chance of finding a great man, know thine enemy: the younger-looking woman! You may have to fight like a tiger against those few extra pounds and gray hairs, but you can do it if you choose to. OR, our little secret, become the younger woman! Be prepared to date older men… they just might treat you like the goddess you truly are!

THE 60 AND OVER GROUP

GETTING OLDER HAS MANY ADVANTAGES. I'M STILL AS IMPERFECT AS EVER, BUT I NO LONGER CARE.

It is considerably more challenging to find quality men for women who are 60 and over. As we saw in Chapter 2, the single men simply aren't there in this age bracket. The higher the socio-economic demographic of the woman, (assuming she wants to meet someone of her status or higher) the more difficult it is to find an appropriate male. Don't forget that there are three times as many single women as men in this age group. Partly this can be attributed to shorter life expectancy for males, but it's also because of men dating and marrying younger women: women under 60.

Lifestyle and life-stage is a huge consideration for this group. Probably for more than any other group, lifestyle and life-stage are key factors. Some people in this group are still very active in their careers, others are retired but still very physically active, and others are retired and not very active.

There seem to be lots of women between 60 and 65 who are very intelligent, successful professionals who are still working full-time. Some of these women are working because they can't afford to retire yet. Others are working because they love what they do and just aren't ready to give it up. Because men tend to be looking for younger women, even if it's only women who are two to five years younger than they are, many of the men who would be looking at women in this age group are already retired and are living a very different lifestyle. Many working women in this group say it doesn't suit them to date men who are retired. These men have expectations that the women just can't meet. The men are looking for someone who can go to lunch with them whenever they want, can take off and golf in the middle of the day Monday through Friday, and can travel with them at the drop of a hat.

Men who are retired also say that they're looking for someone who isn't working and has lots of freedom and flexibility, like they do. A perfect example of this is a 66-year-old retired man who had had a very successful career and was financially well off. He had a winter home in Florida and a summer home in the north. He was looking for a woman ideally between 50 and 60 who was intelligent, classy, well educated, and financially stable. He also wanted this woman to be able to go back and forth between his two homes with him multiple times per year. There were seven women with whom Gloria could match him who fit most of the criteria. The challenge was that five of these seven women were still working full-time and didn't have the flexibility he was looking for.

More than in any other group, the activity level of individuals can vary dramatically and have a huge impact on one's lifestyle. Energy level and attitude about life—slowing down, or moving forward and keeping going—play a major role in finding an appropriate partner.

The other big challenge for this group is that women don't want to become nurses. They don't want to end up taking care of an old man. They want to make sure the man they are going to be with is healthy and youthful. Women in this age range generally want to meet a man who is no more than just a few years older than they are, if not younger. Of course men over 60 are usually looking for a woman who is considerably younger than they are. As much as none of us wants to think about it, or admit it, this group is definitely facing their own mortality. Both men and women are looking for that partner who is ideally going to outlive them. Some of these people are widows or widowers; they know the pain of losing a loved one, and they don't want to have to go through this experience again.

Our Analysis: Betty's Story

For many reasons, Thelma holds up her mother-in-law, Betty Beam, as a model of what life can be like at this age. Betty was married to her husband for about forty years, raised four children, went to college, and had a career. In her sixties, her husband was diagnosed with cancer and passed away after a brief illness. Betty soldiered on, and decided that it was now or never to do some of the things she always wanted to do but never could before. She booked a trip to Australia, and while she was there, she met a man who lived just fifteen minutes away from her house. She really liked him, and they hooked up. Back home, there were some integration issues with the grown-up children. They coped with that and decided not to marry, but to maintain separate residences. Betty had always liked to travel, and so did he. They went to the Caribbean, to Europe, and to Africa. Then, living in a great big house all alone got to be too much for her, but she definitely didn't want to remarry. Betty sold the house and moved into a smaller and cozier condominium in her new beau's building. He lives downstairs and they see each other every day, while maintaining their independence and their own space. When you see them together, they are like two teenagers in love. You wouldn't know they were both in their seventies now.

. . . .

The moral of this story is FLEXIBILITY. This is the very same thing that people begin to lose as they get older. We become set in our ways. We have our own way of doing things, and don't want to change that for anyone. We like what we like and that's that. Our home becomes our castle. We don't want to see anything thrown out or moved around. It becomes hard for us to make adjustments to include another person in our lives.

Guess what? Other people like to have things their own way too. If you can maintain a certain amount of flexibility in all things, then you greatly increase your chances of finding a good man. We mean that you should *be open to new things*, including:

- Where you will live
- Whether or not to travel
- Meeting his family and friends
- Who will pay for what
- Eating out or cooking in
- Hobbies and interests that you do together.

~ **LAW OF THE JUNGLE** ~

If you truly want to increase your statistically low odds of finding a great man, be wide open to all kinds of possibilities. Flexibility is the key! AND, an extra little tip from us: your fellow female competitors in the jungle are generally way too chicken to try any kind of online dating or dating services. If you've got the guts, make sure you find a very reputable service and go for it! It will give you an edge.

THE SERIAL MONOGAMIST GROUP

The women in the Serial Monogamist group are not age-specific. They span a wide range of ages. But no matter what age they are, they have very similar attributes. Typically, they've had a series of one-year to three-year relationships throughout their lives. Even so, most of them have never been married. If they have ever been married, it was one very brief marriage, usually when they were quite young. This group of women has no trouble meeting men. They have no trouble dating men. They can flirt, and use non-verbal communication, and create rapport like pros, (just like we're going to teach you to do in Chapter 9). They really don't have any trouble getting into relationships. They just haven't found "the right one." They've been "unlucky in love." They keep "choosing the wrong men." They're often doing on-line dating, speed-dating, and singles events, as well as using a dating service. They may have tried various dating services.

It's not unusual for these women to be frustrated with the whole dating scene. They've tried everything and nothing has been successful for them. From their experiences the guys on online dating sites aren't looking for a serious relationship; the men who come to speed dating events are dweebs; other singles events have far more women than men (they've met a lot of great women at those events); the dating services keep sending them matches that are so far off; and generally the men they're meeting are losers and jerks. Despite their negative experiences and attitudes they're *still* looking for that elusive Prince Charming.

Our Analysis

Serial Monogamists seem to be handicapped by a number of issues.

Here is one problem faced by Serial Monogamists: they know how to date, but they don't know how to *be in a relationship* with a man. Dating is much different from being married, living together, or just being seriously involved. You have to be pretty committed in order to endure the day-to-day stresses of living with a creature from Mars. If it weren't instinctually programmed, how many women would choose it? And there IS a real art to it, which serial monogamists have not deciphered. They have mastered the art of finding men, but not the art of being with one.

Another problem is that Serial Monogamists have no trouble finding men, but it's always likely to be the SAME man over and over again. That is, there is something about all the men they find which triggers a "run" response. At the same time, *they are only attracted to this type of man.* It's a Catch-22. More will be said on this important issue, which many women share to a greater or lesser extent, in Chapter 6. Read on...

Unless these women are willing to sit back and take serious stock of what they might be doing to contribute to their own situation, they will probably continue in a never-ending series of short-term relationships.

If you think you are a Serial Monogamist, make sure you read Chapter 6—Sabotage of Love. You have some serious issues that you need to deal with before you should try to attain your romantic ideal.

✑ LAW OF THE JUNGLE ✑

If you're a Serial Monogamist and want a fighting chance of KEEPING a man, you may have to do some serious self-reflection and analysis and figure out what's going on. You definitely have to read Chapter 6, but you may have to do a lot more.

THE ELUSIVE LOVE GROUP

Like the Serial Monogamists, this group of women also spans across all age ranges. However, unlike the Serial Monogamists, these women can be in their forties, fifties, and even sixties and they've had no *really* significant romantic relationships in their lives. They've often had one short-term relationship (it could even have been a marriage) that lasted only for a year or two. Very often this one relationship wasn't healthy. This one man in their lives was never really committed to the relationship or to them.

These women have a very difficult time meeting men. They rarely go out on dates. The women who find love and relationships to be apparently completely elusive to them, are just as attractive, fit, intelligent, and financially stable as the women in any of the other five groups. They say "It just hasn't happened for me," or "I just haven't met the right one."

Elusive Love women generally feel that it's incredibly difficult to even meet men. Unlike the Serial Monogamists, they are not out there trying every possible venue to meet that special someone. This group of women generally feels uncomfortable using any of these "artificial" methods of meeting men. They probably aren't overly comfortable flirting. They just don't understand why they need to flirt. They feel flirting is fake, phony, and just not them. Elusive Love women are often introverted, and although they may be warm, loving, wonderful people, they don't come across this way in a first or second date. They may appear to be cool, cold, or even frigid.

One 50-year-old woman who falls into this group says she is a "slow burn." She's not flashy, bubbly, or charismatic. She says that it will take a man a while to get to know her. She feels that this is just who she is, and the man that will love her will have to love her just as she is. The fact is that we are all pretty much who we are, and for the most part, these zebras are not going to change their stripes. People do need to love us for who we are. But this is very much like wanting to find a job. If you really want that job of your dreams, you'll rewrite and spruce up your resume, you'll look through the classified ads, you'll go online to post your resume and look at various listings, you'll connect with headhunters, you'll network, you may go through some career counseling, you may even need to learn how to interview well. You can be a fantastic employee and very knowledgeable in your field, but if you're really horrible in an interview situation, you may have to learn how to interview to get the job that you're worthy of having. It's just like learning how to flirt. Sometimes you just have to do it.

Stacey's Story

Stacey is a 43-year-old woman who is attractive, slim, and fit. She has a very good career as a vice president of a large national corporation, she owns her own home, and is financially stable. She's never had any type of significant relationship. Gloria has introduced her to five or six men. She never gets past the first date. Feedback from her dates was consistent: they found her to be cold, like there was no warmth in her. One man even said "There's no blood running in those veins." That isn't true, but she obviously was not coming across well in the meetings with new men. If she wants to increase her chances of getting one of these men to be attracted to her, she's going to have to learn how to show some of her warmth, be slightly more vivacious and open, and even learn how to flirt on that first meeting.

. . . .

The women in this group work really hard at feeling complete and whole within themselves. They've built up a great group of female friends, but somehow it's just not enough. In their down moments they ask themselves "Why me? Why hasn't it happened for me yet? Will it *ever* happen for me?"

⤿ LAW OF THE JUNGLE ⤾

If you always do what you've always done, you'll always get what you've always gotten. In order to get what you've never gotten, you've got to do what you've never done! In other words, you're going to have to walk out on a limb, take a big risk, and change something. Maybe just go crazy and learn how to flirt!

Our Analysis

PLEASE DON'T HURT ME.

Whenever someone *says* she wants something very badly, but doesn't seem to be able to get it, or only tries half-heartedly to get it, then you have to ask what she is getting out of NOT having it.

As the great psychoanalyst Sigmund Freud said, very often, our greatest wish is also our greatest fear. This often leaves people paralyzed, not knowing what to do. If your greatest wish is to be in a serious long-term relationship with a man, it could lead to many things. It might mean that you would have a shoulder to lay your head on at night; a home and family of your own; security; and love. It could also mean that you might fail at these things; that you might have to open yourself up to another person; that you don't feel that you deserve to have all the good things that would come from a relationship. In that case your greatest wish could also be your greatest fear. The power of human beings to protect themselves and their ego from possible harm cannot be overstated.

Most of our fears are learned and reinforced as children. If you had parents, or even one parent, who made you feel that you were a screw-up, or that you didn't deserve to have things because of some character flaw; or that relationships were frightening for some reason, or that sex was bad, or that the other person will leave, this might have been the origin of your fears. Or maybe a previous past relationship was so awful or ended so badly that you feel unequal to the task of repeating the experiment … The list of possible causes goes on and on. The point is that you need to do some serious soul searching, just as much as the Serial Monogamist group, about *what exactly it is that you're afraid of* when it comes to men or being in a relationship. These fears tend to be very deep, very difficult to get at just by thinking about it. But unless you can figure this out, maybe with the help of a qualified professional, then you may find that you are constantly sabotaging yourself, even with the nicest men.

If you find yourself in the Elusive Love group, make sure you pay particular attention to Chapter 6—Sabotage of Love, and Chapter 9—How Men Hunt Today.

Chapter 5

What Men Want

First Impressions

"It all depends on how we look at things, and not on how they are themselves."

Here is a game that we sometimes play with an audience when giving a seminar. Try it yourself when you are among strangers. The subway is perfect, or the grocery checkout line. It will relieve some boredom while you're waiting.

When you're in a place full of strangers, take a look around you. Now, out of all the people that you see, which one of them is most likely...

1. To sing in the shower?

2. To be in love?

3. To listen to classical music?

4. To be cheating on their spouse?

5. To walk around the house in their underwear?

Well? Did you identify a person for each question above? If you did, you can see that people (including you) can make judgments all the time, usually with little or no evidence. AND we make them intuitively. If we didn't have this ability, we would never be able to sense when someone around us poses a danger or an opportunity.

We are bringing this fact to your attention because we so often hear women say that they don't want to be judged based only on a first impression. They want a man to get to know them before making any judgments about them. And they certainly don't want to be judged on the way they look! In doing this, they are asking that a man suspend the normal human process of gathering sensory, nonverbal information on first contact. How he is supposed to do this is not quite clear, but that's what they ideally want. Unfortunately, it's impossible. Impressions will be given and judgments will be made right from the very first contact with you. Your best defense is to make sure that those impressions are good ones.

A good impression starts out with your physical appearance. It is impossible to overstate how much information a man is able to gather just by watching you walking into the restaurant for your blind date. Humans form impressions on the basis of pattern recognition; they are looking to see whether or not you conform to their innate sense of what turns them on. These patterns are as old as the *homo sapiens* species and are hardwired into our brains. A woman sends out nonverbal messages from her age, her face, her energy, the way she looks and dresses, and the gestures she makes. There is a wealth of information here for a man to sense. It happens very very quickly and it is almost completely unconscious.

According to principles of evolutionary psychology, the criteria for how men assess attractiveness are well researched and fall into four categories:[5]

. . . .

5   Nick Neave, "Evolutionary Psychology Lecture 7: Male Mate Preferences"

1. Youth

2. Beauty

3. Health

4. Behavioral Characteristics

All of these characteristics are related to a woman's reproductive value. The fact that men may not consciously desire to
reproduce when they're well into their fifties and beyond makes
no difference to their unconscious criteria for what they find
attractive in a woman. The operative word here is UNCONSCIOUS.
Because all of these criteria are operating at an unconscious level,
it's no good fighting against them. Very often, we hear women
ranting and raving against the superficiality of men. They say
that men are only interested in how they look (yes, and naked if
possible), not the kind of person they are on the inside. This is
not completely true, but it does appear to take men longer to get
at what's inside—they spend so much time looking at the outside.
What women don't seem to understand is that men are operating
instinctively. They can't help it. We suggest that instead of getting
upset about something men have no control over, you USE these
unconscious criteria to your own advantage. Fighting against
unconscious programming is fighting a losing battle. But when you
understand the programming, you can learn to work with it rather
than against it.

Charlotte's Story

Charlotte is a 47-year-old single mother of two teenagers.
She's been divorced for about ten years and has dedicated herself
to raising her kids and promoting her career. Like so many single
moms in this age range, her kids are now at a point where they
pretty much have their own social lives and Charlotte is starting to
think about dating for the first time since her divorce.

The first man we introduced to Charlotte was Steve, a single father with an excellent career, who had raised two daughters on his own since they were quite young. Steve called Charlotte to arrange a time to get together for their first meeting. According to Steve, the conversation was going quite well and he thought Charlotte sounded fun and interesting. Charlotte then asked Steve what the next step was. Steve suggested that they should set up a time to get together to see if there was any attraction. With this, Charlotte went ballistic. She asked Steve what he would consider attractive. He told her that he was looking for someone who was slim, reasonably fit, and a non-smoker.

Charlotte called us in a fury. She didn't want to meet any man who was just going to be meeting her to see if he was "attracted" to her. She didn't want some man who was going to be looking at her body. She only wanted to meet men who truly cared about who she was as a person, who she was on the inside, not the outside. The amazing thing is that Charlotte is very slim, petite, and fit, and she's a non-smoker. Everything Steve said he was looking for.

. . . .

Why do some women reject their outward appearance and say it's not a part of who they are? What makes the outside any less a part of us than the inside? The physical body can become the "shadow," the part of ourselves which we wish to disavow and hide. Except it's really hard to do that when it's the first thing that people see. Some women expect a man to have the same distorted view of their identity as they do, so they don't want a man to notice them physically. This is impossible. In Charlotte's case, her total disconnection from her body was not Steve's fault, but he sure triggered some powerful emotions around this sensitive issue!

⤷ LAW OF THE JUNGLE ⤶
Don't fight against nature. Work with it.

Psychological research has found that, regardless of their own age, men instinctively look for women with a high reproductive value. Unfortunately for men, the reproductive value of the human female is not usually on display, but men, over the course of countless generations, have learned to look for certain clues. The first and most obvious clue is youth. Remember what the statistics showed, that many men coming back into the relationship market are snapped up by younger women? If it makes you feel better, there is actually a scientific reason for this.

Women reach their reproductive peak around the age of 20, and then it declines steadily and rapidly after that. Now, you would think that as men age, they wouldn't care about the reproductive value in having a young wife, and they don't, not consciously anyway. But cross-cultural research has shown that men generally prefer younger wives,[6] and, even as they age, they prefer mates who are increasingly younger than themselves.[7]

Men's Age Preferences

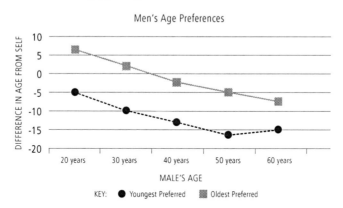

There is some good news here, though. For short-term relationships and sexual fantasies, men prefer mates who are at the peak of reproductive ability, between the ages of 18 and 30.

....

6   David M. Buss, "Sex differences in human mate preferences: Evolutionary hypotheses tested in 37 cultures," *Behavioral and Brain Sciences*, 12:1-49.

7   Kenrick, D.T. and R.C. Keefe, "Age preferences in mates reflect sex differences in mating strategies," Behavioral & Brain Sciences, 15: 75-91

However, for long-term relationships, men prefer women who, although still younger than themselves, could be past the age of fertility.[8] This may not be so much their own preference, but a fact of nature: young women don't generally go for old geezers (unless of course, they have lots of money).

You see, there is a scientific reason for why we advise you to become the younger woman and consider dating men who are ten to fifteen years older than yourself.

Okay, so you're not young. You're over 40. Should you just concede defeat to the younger women? Absolutely not! But don't step into the trap that so many women fall into, which is deluding themselves that they look younger than they really are.

Recently, we received the following email in response to an advertisement placed in a local paper:

> "My age is above the stated criteria, as I am 52. As an active, healthy, athletic person, my real age according to realage.com is 43."

And then we get no end of comments such as:

> "I'm 56, but all my friends tell me I look ten to twelve years younger than I am."

> "I'm an incredibly youthful 51, I don't look or act my age."

> "I'm 49, but I don't look a day over 39."

We hear these things with monotonous regularity from both men and women.

If you hear yourself saying any of the above, give your head a shake. Don't fool yourself. It's NOT true. You're probably saying right now, "Well, but I really DO look ten years younger than I am." We are here to tell you that you're delusional. If we added the words "I'd like to think" in front of any of the above statements—"I'm

---

8   Nick Neave, "Evolutionary Psychology Lecture 7: Male Mate Preferences"

49, but I'd like to think I don't look at day over 39"—that might be more accurate.

Of the hundreds of men and women we've interviewed in the past several years, nine out of ten of them say they're much younger-looking, younger-feeling, and younger-acting then they are. This "youthful outlook" is a well-known phenomenon. Basically, when people reach middle age, they still tend to think and see themselves as ten to fifteen years younger than they really are. When they look in the mirror, they don't see a 55-year-old face. They see a face that's 40 or 45. Marketers use this optical illusion to advertise to Baby Boomers. See for yourself, the next time you are looking through a catalogue or a print ad for a store that is obviously targeted to mature women. How old are the models? Are they in their fifties? Or do they look closer to 35 or 40?

Matt Thornhill, who runs The Boomer Project, a research and consulting firm in Richmond, Virginia, has spent several years studying attitudinal characteristics of the Boomer generation. His research shows that Boomers see themselves as twelve years younger on average than they are. Boomers over 50 see themselves as about 14 years younger than they are. So 52 is the new 38.

The moral of the story is: *Do NOT delude yourself!* You look your age, maybe even older! But take heart, all your peers are right there with you.

It used to be that men were the ones who wanted women ten years or more younger than them. Now plenty of women are *also* saying they want to meet men younger then they are. Do the math. It just doesn't work. We all can't date someone ten years younger than we are. Actually, statistics show that while some men may date someone ten to twenty years younger than they are, they usually end up marrying, or being in a long-term relationship with someone much closer to their own age.

Gloria's Story

The first man I ever met when I started my dating service was 46 years old, turning 47 in just two months. He said he wanted to meet a woman between 30 and 40 years old. He had dated a 29-year-old and a 25-year-old. He ended up with a woman who is just eight months younger than he is. Me! I tease him about how he really robbed the cradle. After all, when I was in diapers, he was in looser diapers. (When we were infants, there was no such thing as different sized disposable diapers. Our mothers just had to loosen the safety pins.)

. . . .

The next major hurdle is Beauty, which is important because it is a clue to one's general health, just as Youth is. Why beauty? Just think about it. Are you attracted to men when they have the flu and are coughing and sneezing everywhere? Do you go for guys that have a sallow complexion or who have open sores on their face? These things are all indications of disease, and we instinctively shy away from them, as do other mammals.[9] So do men. Instinctively, they want women who look young because young women are more likely to be healthy and fertile. An attractive woman is a healthy woman. At an unconscious level, beauty provides a clue to youth and health, and therefore to reproductive value. The things that men find attractive are also the things that may indicate a woman's age and whether or not she is healthy: smooth skin, bright eyes, red lips, glossy hair.[10]

To some extent, the concept of beauty is cultural. For instance, in North American society, thin is in, whereas in some African societies, chubbiness is an indicator of nutrition, affluence, and health and therefore considered very attractive. We have also seen

. . . .

9 Schaller, Mark and Lesley A. Duncan, "The behavioral immune system: Its evolution and social psychological implications," in *Evolution and the Social Mind: Evolutionary Psychology and Social Cognition*. New York: Psychology Press.

10 Nick Neave, "Evolutionary Psychology Lecture 7: Male Mate Preferences"

that the concept of beauty changes over time, just like fashion. One of the things that doesn't change over time, though, is male preferences for body shape. The most attractive female figure type is the hourglass figure. It is possible to have this shape even if you are not thin, because the important component is the waist-to-hip ratio. A waist-to-hip ratio of 0.7 is considered ideal. It may also interest you to know that Audrey Hepburn and Marilyn Monroe had the same waist-to-hip ratio of 0.7. Both women are considered to be very attractive, even though they have very different body types.[11]

TOUCH YOUR NOSE TO A FULL LENGTH MIRROR, TAKE A TINY STEP BACK AND LOOK DOWN. WHAT YOU SEE IS YOUR SWEETHEART'S INTIMATE VIEW.

Related to body shape, the biggest issue for women over 40, even more than looking their age, is their weight. We are assuming that many of you are either overweight or out of shape. If you are,

. . . .
11   Burnham, Terry, and Jay Phelan, *Mean Genes*, Penguin Books, 2001, pg 162.

you're in good company. Between the ages of 45 and 54, three-quarters of American men and two-thirds of American women are overweight, and about half of those fall into the definition of "obese." By the time women are between 55 and 64, they have swelled even more, and now almost three-quarters of them are overweight.

PERCENTAGE OF U.S. MEN AND WOMEN WHO ARE OVERWEIGHT

	Men	Women
35 – 44 years of age	71%	61%
45 – 54 years of age	76%	65%
55 – 64 years of age	75%	72%
65 – 74 years of age	76%	71%

Source: U.S. Census - Health 2004

If, when you look at yourself naked in the mirror you see something like a potato shape, then it is time to focus some effort on your form. You don't need to become anorexic-looking, but you do need to start eating better and going to the gym. Most men are *visual* and want to date a woman who looks good and healthy. As discussed, physical attractiveness is far more important to men than it is to women. It doesn't matter that they themselves may look like Humpty Dumpty. Relationship economics favor the men, so it is necessary for you to make yourself as attractive as possible, because this is what they are looking for—or else they'll search for a younger woman. It's as brutal as that, but if you remember, it's the law of the jungle.

❧ LAW OF THE JUNGLE ❧

Men are visual and life isn't fair. You have to look as good as you can because you're competing with younger women all the time.

When it comes to attractiveness, the face is an important component. A beautiful face is a symmetrical face, in both men and women. In judging faces, the unconscious mind looks for symmetry and evidence of youthfulness: large eyes, high cheek bones, small nose, small chin, full lips.[12] If you don't have a perfectly symmetrical and unblemished face, then we have a word for you: Makeup! We don't mean that you should make yourself up like an old tart, but a dab of makeup, judiciously applied, can give the impression of youth and health and thus satisfy these unconscious but important male criteria. If you are not sure how to apply makeup for this effect, you have only to look to your local department store for help. Very often the aestheticians there can show you how to apply the products for maximum effect.

Recently we received some feedback from a man on a woman to whom we had introduced him. He said he liked her, she was interesting and intelligent, but that she just wasn't feminine enough. When we questioned him on what he meant by that, he said she wasn't wearing any makeup. He said he liked a woman who wore some makeup, just enough to look natural. In this case, this was the only thing he could articulate that wasn't "right" for him with this woman. It was enough to keep him from calling her a second time. Numerous men have made comments to us about liking a woman who wears a bit of makeup.

Of course, by now you know that there is a scientific reason for this, don't you? Makeup enables average-looking women to create a more healthy and youthful appearance. Makeup allows a woman to make her face more symmetrical, even out her skin tone, and exaggerate features like eyes and lips. All of these things are subconscious cues to the male of the woman's youthfulness and health. At a conscious level, it indicates to them that she's sexually receptive, is trying to make herself attractive for him, takes care of

....

12   Nick Neave, "Evolutionary Psychology Lecture 7: Male Mate Preferences"

herself, and will continue to take care of herself as she gets older. So makeup is important.

Finally, look at your teeth. Yellow teeth are not only unattractive, but they make you look older. There are a number of excellent products available for whitening your teeth, and you should take advantage of these.

Next, take a look at your wardrobe. Is there anything to tickle a man's fancy in there or is your closet full of severe business suits and sensible shoes? Do you have eighteen pairs of jeans and/or stretchy exercise pants? Are turtlenecks *de rigueur* as both day and eveningwear? Do you feel uncomfortable unless you are wearing several layers that cover you up completely? Do you go grocery shopping in your track suit? If you are guilty of any of these crimes of fashion, then a makeover is definitely called for. Again, you do NOT have to look like you just stepped out of the pages of *Vogue*. But you should look clean and well put together, with a sense of your own mature style.

We suggest you ask your friends for help here or hire a professional image consultant. It really doesn't have to cost you a fortune. If finding a partner is a high priority in your life, it's an investment that could really pay off. We've had clients who have been amazed at the change in response they get from the opposite sex after working with an image consultant for just a couple of sessions. They may have changed their hairstyle a bit, purchased new glasses, or changed a few things in their wardrobe. Get either a friend (make sure it's someone who doesn't have the exact same taste and style as you do), or a professional to go through your closet and fish out items that make you look fat, dumpy, older, or out-of-date. Then get rid of those things and go shopping. To prevent you from just buying more of the things you already have, we encourage you to take someone along whose taste and style you respect. Shop to make the absolute best of who you are right now. Don't shop for who you might be when you're twenty pounds slimmer right after you start that diet! Trust us, it is extremely unlikely that you will ever be young enough or thin enough to wear those stiletto heels and red miniskirt again. But every woman should have a little black dress and some fine lingerie. When you get dressed up to meet a man do you feel good about yourself? Do you feel feminine and even just a bit sexy? If you don't feel this way, how is *he* going to feel this way about you?

I KEEP THIS IN MY CLOSET JUST TO TORTURE MYSELF.

Since men use shape as one clue about a woman's attractive-ness, it won't help you to cover yourself up like a tent. We find that many women, of both normal and above normal weight, tend to dress in layers of clothes that hide their shape. Layers of clothes may make you feel secure, but they will only confuse him. Men have actually complained that when they met a woman who was wearing a suit they couldn't tell a thing about what she looked like! To the man this means he didn't know what the woman was like as a person. We tend to look at faces to understand who the man is. Men look at a body to understand who the woman is. To a man, the more clothes you have on, the bigger and more shapeless you look, therefore the less attractive. Try something that is relaxed but still indicates that you have a womanly shape under there.

✑ LAW OF THE JUNGLE ✑
When he looks at you, he should see a woman. In your dating preparedness makeover, place special emphasis on those clues to your womanliness which men instinctively look for.

Finally, men unconsciously look for certain behavioral characteristics when assessing a woman's mate potential. One of those characteristics is sexual availability.

In a world where the single women far outnumber single men their own age, you would think that offering sex would be a cost of entry into the relationship market (more will be said on this in Chapter 10—The Big Question), but actually, men are programmed at an unconscious level to look for mates who are faithful and not promiscuous.[13] However, women who are promiscuous may still be considered as potential sexual partners without prejudice.

In this book we're addressing the issues of dating and we're making the assumption that you're looking for a romantic, and therefore sexual, relationship. Our biggest issue with women over 40 is that they're giving out too many non-sexual messages. We're not for a second suggesting that you start draping yourself all over the man the first time you meet for coffee. This would be strongly giving him the message that you're looking for sex only. But your appearance and gestures should indicate that you MIGHT be avail-

. . . .
13 Ibid

able for sex under the right circumstances and for the right man. You have to look, feel and act feminine and somewhat sexy—note that doesn't mean slutty. In short, you have to know how to flirt. We'll discuss the art of flirting in Chapter 9—How Men Hunt Today.

Other desirable behavioral characteristics are also related to reproductive value. Survival traits such as intelligence, kindness, empathy, ability to nurture, a positive and optimistic attitude, energy, a sense of humor, the ability to communicate nonverbally: all are important. Exhibiting these characteristics can work to your advantage in triggering the male's unconscious program.

WOMEN'S PREFERENCES FOR MEN

In case you are feeling righteous about how female mate preferences are obviously more highly evolved than men's because they are not so focussed on the physical, we thought it might be a good idea to go into the evolutionary psychology of what women find attractive about men. When it comes to mating and childrearing, one thing is obvious: our ancestors, just like women today, had to put a lot of time and effort into attracting a suitable mate, being pregnant, and then rearing a child. It's a big investment for them. They want to make sure that their offspring survive and thrive, so women have evolved to prefer mates who will make the investment worthwhile:

1. Partners that can provide a range of resources including food, shelter, and protection

2. Partners who have a high social status and are looked up to by other men

3. Physical health and beauty.[14]

---

14 Dr. Nick Neave, "Evolutionary Psychology Lecture 6: Female Mate Preferences."

Again, these preferences have *evolved over eons* because they contribute to the health and happiness of women and their offspring. Women can't help noticing a man in a Hugo Boss suit and Rolex watch any more than men can help noticing a young woman with big breasts. And these preferences do not extinguish simply because you are menopausal. They apply to older couples, even when it doesn't make any sense in terms of reproduction. Obviously, two 50-year-olds are not going to try to start a family together. Unfortunately, your reptilian brain, the one that is about instincts and survival, doesn't know that and couldn't care less.

There has also been a lot of research done around female mate preferences which suggests that the kind of man they seek is directly related to their ovulation cycle.[15] Wow! Just think about that! Maybe you chose that handsome but no-good, womanizing, arrogant son-of-a-bitch when you were ovulating, and then regretted it a few days later. Another research study has found that women dress in a way to make themselves more attractive to men when they are ovulating.[16] What this means is that a lot of women's mate preferences and behavior is *also* guided by evolutionary pressures that they are not aware of. Women simply evolved differently from men. Just differently, not better.

One of the reasons that young women marry older men is because these partners are more likely to be able to provide "resources" and status. If they are older, they have probably already established themselves financially and are in a position to take care of a family. A partner's ability to provide financial security is more important to women than to men. At Perfect Partners, nine out of ten women mention income or assets as a very important criterion,

15   For instance, see Pilsworth, Elizabeth G., "Ovulatory shifts in female sexual desire" in *Journal of Sex Research*, February 2004, or Simpson, Jeffry A. and Jonathon Lapaglia, "*Strategic Pluralism and Human mating: Patterned changes in women's mate preferences across the ovulatory cycle.*" Preliminary draft, January 2005.

16   Maggie Fox, "Fertility fuels fashion" in www.thecouriermail.news.com.au reports on research conducted by Dr. Martie Haselton for UCLA.

whereas nine out of ten men say it is unimportant in a potential partner. Even women who are extremely well-off, or independently wealthy, and could very easily afford to support a man, are looking for a man who makes about as much money as they do or MORE. They do not want to support a man financially. Whereas any man we've met who is in a similar financial position, would have no problem supporting a woman.

THE MYTH OF THE THREATENING FEMALE

Success is so important to women in assessing a man's desirability that they do not understand it when a successful man "dates down" by dating a well-endowed bimbo rather than an intelligent, educated, and successful professional woman. This is incomprehensible and crazy-making, so women try to rationalize it to themselves. For instance, we have heard women say that men are "threatened" by their success.

Lately, we have seen a positive rash of "Cinderella" movies, where a highly successful man prefers the maid, dog walker, the tea lady, the office intern, a prostitute with a golden heart, or some other lower status female to a woman who is their social equal. Women of a high social status are portrayed as stuck-up bitches and nags.

We, however, do not believe that most men are threatened by a woman's success. In his wonderfully insightful book *What Women Want – What Men Want*, John Townsend describes an experiment conducted with men and women who were asked to look at attractive and homely models dressed in different outfits:

"The high-status costume consisted of a white dress shirt with a designer paisley tie, a navy blazer thrown over the left shoulder, and a Rolex wrist watch. Female models wore a white silk blouse, a navy blazer thrown over the left shoulder, and a woman's Rolex. To depict medium status, models wore an off-white shirt and khaki slacks. For low social

status the models wore the uniform of a well-known hamburger chain: a baseball cap and a polo shirt with the company logo showing. Male and female models were matched for physical attractiveness." [17]

Women tended to choose the high-status model regardless of how physically attractive he was for all types of relationships, including meeting for coffee, dating, sexual relations, and marriage. The men were much more democratic; they didn't care what outfit the prettiest model wore, she was picked most often for all types of relationships. Furthermore, when asked to rate the models' physical attractiveness, the costumes affected the women's ratings but not the men's. It's like the men could look right through the costumes and visualize the model naked. Women, on the other hand, had to be able to visualize what the model could give them or do for them, and this was the main component of how women judged their attractiveness.

Townsend concludes that a woman's social status is neither here nor there to a man in evaluating her desirability for sex or relationship. For men, "dating down," if such a concept exists, would mean dating someone unattractive. For a woman, dating down is a real concept and means dating below your own social status. It is this difference in perception that explains why Cinderella movies are so popular with both men and women. Women like these stories because Cinderella is dating up, which gives them hope that any girl will be able to attract a Prince Charming. And for men, as one of our respondents told us, *"Cinderella is always a babe."*

Again, we can't help it. That's the way we have evolved. Our ancestors who chose men who were not good providers did not have as many children survive, so we can't help desiring a man for what he can materially provide. To be a bit crass, men look at beauty the way women look at bank accounts. A man marries a woman for her youth and beauty, just like a woman marries a man

17   Townsend, John, *What Women Want – What Men Want: Why The Sexes Still See Love & Commitment So Differently,* Oxford University Press, New York, 1998, pg. 63

for his money and status. Now, before you say "Oh, that's not me," check yourself. Ask yourself this question: Is the income range of a potential partner important to you? We've never heard a woman say an unequivocal "no." In fact, it seems that the more money the woman has, the more money she wants the man to have. This isn't logical, it's not necessarily reasonable, but it is instinctual. Even if we don't need a man to support us, we want a man who *could* support us.

Almost as important as income or assets is occupation. So many women say they want a man with a profession or a business executive. This is because traditionally, financial wealth and status have been correlated with education and occupation. Very few men we interviewed cared much what a woman does for a living (as long as she's got big breasts—kidding!). Hard-working men definitely make women feel more secure, so industriousness and success are valuable assets in a mate.

Finally, physical attractiveness is not totally unimportant either. Women also want men who appear to be healthy, which means not too old, with big but not huge shoulders, no beer belly, and a symmetrical face. In terms of height, in general women prefer men who are taller than themselves, but who fall into an "average" height category.[18] However, men can be quite a bit older without being "too old," since men are fertile a lot longer than women are. Nor can fertility be evaluated just from looking at a man.

So you see, biology is destiny. Blame your genes.

While we've just addressed how you look —what's going on on the outside, there is another equally important aspect to look at in preparing to date—what's going on on the inside. What are you thinking and how are you feeling? Where are you emotionally?

. . . .

18 Ibid

TO PREVENT FUTURE DISAPPOINTMENT, I ALWAYS
GO ON A FIRST DATE LOOKING LIKE I WOULD
AFTER WE'VE LIVED TOGETHER FOR SEVERAL YEARS

Chapter 6

Sabotage of Love

In addition to your outward appearance, there are probably some emotional issues you will have to deal with before you can begin dating. There are so many good reasons not to take a chance on a relationship and so many things that can go wrong and break your heart, that it is not surprising that most of us, to one extent or another, attempt to sabotage love.

Sabotage of love manifests in a number of different ways, most notably:

1. Unresolved feelings for your ex

2. Dating the same type of person over and over again

3. Ambivalence about being in a romantic relationship.

Let's start with the most obvious, having unresolved feelings for your ex, or, even worse, still being in love with him. Love is not a rational emotion, and cannot be directed towards a particular object. That's why we call it "falling" in love, indicating that you lose all sense of control when you're in it.

In Love with Your Ex

Okay, so you find yourself still in love with your ex, or not able to focus your emotions on another person because your ex still dominates your thoughts and feelings. Or you had a wonderful twenty-year relationship with your true soulmate who passed away suddenly four years ago. What do you do?

a. Pull out all the stops and get back together with him (assuming he's still in the land of the living) to give it another shot.

b. Force yourself not to think about him and focus on getting a new man in your life.

c. Find someone who reminds you of your ex and makes you feel the same fuzzy-wuzzy way.

d. Find someone who is the exact opposite of your ex.

e. Clean out his stuff from your closets, put away the photos and keepsakes, and resolve your feelings before trying to get into another serious relationship.

The correct answer, of course, is (e). You cannot force yourself to stop loving someone. You cannot successfully replace one man with a clone. He's not a goldfish that has just died. And purposely finding someone totally different is like running away from your emotions. No, there is no easy way to do this, you must simply come to some kind of understanding and resolution about what happened: the good, the bad, and the ugly.

Julie's Story

Julie, an intelligent, beautiful woman had been in love with Adam for more than eight years. He said he loved her too. The problem was that every time they got together, the same issues would emerge, quarrels would ensue, and they would be forced apart once again. Julie was determined to leave this relationship behind because she wanted to be married and have a family, and she knew that this would never happen in this on-again, off-again relationship. She dated many men, and eventually met one who seemed to fulfill all of the things she wanted in a partner. Things went well for a while, but the relationship failed. She found that she could not stop thinking about Adam. Finally, after a year of therapy, she felt that she had learned enough about herself to give it one last try. Julie began getting close to Adam, more slowly this time, and they shared at a much more intimate level than they ever had before. She really had grown! She had discovered many things about herself and was investing the patience to make the relationship with Adam finally work. But Adam had not. Emotionally, he was still back where he was when they last broke up. She had been using the time apart for self improvement and awareness, but he hadn't. Soon, the same types of problems began to surface. Julie handled them with new-found maturity. Adam didn't. And although it broke her heart, Julie finally understood that this relationship was NEVER going to work. Even if she had been smarter, prettier, more organized, more talented—whatever—their differences were just too great. And finally, ten years after first meeting Adam, she was able to let him go. Was she sorry she had wasted this time on a seemingly hopeless cause? No, she was sure now that Adam was not the man for her; she would never have to ask "What if?" And, while there would always be a part of her that loved him, she was no longer *in love* with him and was free to focus her attention elsewhere.

. . . .

That's how it is sometimes. You just have to do something over and over again until you get it right. In Julie's case, the right thing was to say goodbye to Adam, and eventually, she got it. Maybe you also feel that you have to try to get your ex back. We will not judge you if you do, but for heaven's sake, do it with your eyes open. For most of you, however, some serious self-reflection, preferably with the help of a qualified professional, may be enough to set you free. Especially if your ex has remarried or otherwise moved on.

Gretchen's Story

Gretchen had been married for fifteen years to an extremely successful man. They enjoyed a wonderful lifestyle together. They owned five homes in various countries, they skied all over the world, and they raised three great children together. Life was great. Until four years ago when Sam suddenly dropped dead of a heart attack. Gretchen was left in shock, with a huge estate that was in a mess!

Gradually, Gretchen was able to make it through the shock and all of the legal mess with the estate. The kids eventually were back up on their feet again, the two oldest ones out of college with successful careers and living on their own, and the youngest one in her last year of high school and now doing well again. It was time for Gretchen to start thinking about herself. She was ready to get out there in the dating game again. After all, it had been four years, and the kids were pretty well on their own now.

So Gretchen called a dating service. During the two-hour interview, Gretchen talked non-stop about her deceased husband. The answer to every question specifically about *her* was answered with a "*we* used to do this," or "*my husband* was a very this or that kind of man," or "well, *my husband* and I," etc., etc. At the end of the interview she asked if it was okay if she still wore her wedding rings when she went on a date. When the answer came back to her that that probably wouldn't be appropriate, and that it would give the man the sense that she wasn't emotionally ready to move on, she was quite surprised. She went on to explain that it wasn't that she wasn't ready to move on, it was just that there was so much fondness there, such wonderful memories, that she didn't feel she should have to give up her rings. After all, no one had to worry. It wasn't like her husband was going to come back. No, that's true, but in Gretchen's mind was he really gone?

. . . .

One more secret: Creating physical space by getting rid of something you no longer need has the effect of creating psychological space. It's like you are putting an intention forth to the Universe that you are ready to fill up your space with something new! Think about how much "space," in your mind and in your heart, your ex is taking up, and clean out a commensurate amount of space in your house and closets (preferably by throwing out his old stuff). Don't try to hang on to anything you no longer need.

✂ LAW OF THE JUNGLE ✂
You cannot be on with the new love until you are off with the old.

DATING THE SAME MAN OVER AND OVER AGAIN

When Bob split from his wife, the first woman he brought home to meet his family made everyone's jaw drop to the floor. The new girlfriend was the spitting image of his ex-wife! The most bizarre thing about it was that Bob couldn't see that he was dating a clone of his ex. When someone pointed out the striking resemblance, Bob said "What do you mean? She doesn't look anything like Rose."

Loss is a powerful emotion which motivates us to replace what has been lost with something as close to it as possible. We encounter all sorts of people, both men and women, who find clones of their ex. Usually this happens at an unconscious level. They are not aware that they have picked a girlfriend called Maria when their ex's name was Mary. Or that she wants a man who is six-feet tall because that's how tall her deceased husband was. Or that he will only date blondes and his ex-wife was a blonde, and so on. These people are dating the same person they lost in different disguises.

We've even seen plenty of cases where people consciously want a clone of their ex. During one interview, when we asked a woman what she wanted in a man, she pulled out a picture of her ex, and asked us to find someone who looked just like him. Looking through her photo album, we could not distinguish one old boyfriend from another: they all had "The Look." Regardless of what other sterling qualities a potential partner might possess, this woman had to have "The Look." We could not bring ourselves to ask who had originally imprinted himself into her psyche so deeply that she could not do without him.

Dating the same person in different disguises is not just about how they look, but how they *feel*. According to Harville Hendrix,[19] author and marriage counselor, we learn all about relationships at an early age, usually before the age of six. We become imprinted with our original role models—usually our parents—and that's how we eventually pick our mates. In order to resolve our conflicts with our parents, we choose partners who make us feel the same way. Our partners are a combination of the best and also the most challenging aspects of our parents. So, for instance, perhaps he has your father's sense of humor, which you love, but he also has your mother's temper, which you hate. But at least it's all familiar.

As with physical attractiveness, emotional attraction is based on pattern recognition. We have an imprint in our hearts of how a partner is supposed to make us feel, and that's what we look for in a person. This is not always a good thing. Many women who

19   Harville Hendrix, *Getting The Love You Want*, HarperPerennial, New York, 1990.

did not have positive male role models in their fathers end up on the therapist's couch in order to understand why they make such poor mating choices. If their fathers were cold, aloof, or absent, they may look for men who are emotionally unavailable and spend their lives trying to get their man's attention. If their fathers were strict disciplinarians, women may look for men who make them feel as though they can do nothing right. If women found themselves in competition with their mothers for Father's attention (the Freudian "Electra Complex"), they may look for love triangles where they have to compete with another woman. Alternately, if Dad was an overachiever, they may be looking for men who live up to this standard but are otherwise unsuitable or unattainable. The unconscious issues that can make a woman become a saboteur of love are innumerable.

Readers who identify with the Serial Monogamist description were specifically directed to this chapter. For you and any other women who seem to date the same person over and over again, you may find some relief in tracing out your "man program." This is how you do it. It might take some time, depending on how many men have been in your life, so you may want to work on it over the course of a few days.

EXERCISE

1. Start a list, beginning with your father and any other significant male relationships you had in your childhood (uncle, grandfather, or brother, especially if he's a twin brother).

2. Write down all the things you loved about each one. Then, write down all the things you really disliked about them.

3. Think about conflicts you had with them and how you dealt with those issues. What did you do? How did you feel?

4. Make a list of all your significant romantic relationships, starting

with your first real boyfriend. Make sure you include the first man you had sex with.

5. Next, take this second list and write down the things you loved about each one, and then the things you hated about them.

6. Trace out the course of each relationship. Who approached whom? Who broke up with whom? What happened to end the relationship? Was there another person involved (not just another romantic attachment but any person who got between you in the relationship, like a mother-in-law or a child)? How long did each last?

When you look at this written record, you should begin to see some similarities. On the outside, all the men may *seem* to be different. Maybe Bill had red hair and Howard had blonde hair. Your father was athletic and David wasn't, and so on. Try to look beyond these traits and see what patterns emerge.

Ruth's Story

Ruth is an attractive, successful businesswoman in her sixties. She was married once, a long time ago, and is still friends with her ex-husband. She came into therapy to understand what had happened in a very serious relationship which had just been broken off. In the course of tracing out her "man program," two important pieces of information came to light: 1) Ruth was the younger daughter, and her mother's favorite, but her father preferred her sister. When she was young Ruth used to sneak her sister's clothes and wear them to go out. 2) In every serious relationship Ruth had had, there was always a triangle with another person. Sometimes, she would fall in love with another man; other times she was replaced by another woman. In the current relationship, Ruth had been competing with an ex-wife, or rather the memory of an ex-wife whom Stan still loved. When she saw this pattern, she realized that Stan was a stand-in for her father, who still preferred her sister. Ruth realized that she chose Stan *because* this love triangle was how she understood love relationships to be: that's what had been imprinted on her from her childhood, longing after a man who preferred another.

. . . .

You might well ask yourself: How is it possible that someone wouldn't notice a pattern as big as always having to be in a love triangle? But these programs all work at an unconscious level. By definition, people aren't aware of them. As an extreme example of just how unconscious these relationship programs are, we can take Matthew, who came into therapy because he needed some clarity on his career. When Matthew traced out his "woman program," there were many patterns. However, the most interesting one happened after he broke up the relationship. Each time a relationship ended, Matthew would literally pack his bags and leave town, and take up residence in another city. This moving around was having a serious impact on his ability to maintain a career, yet remarkably, he was not aware that he moved every single time a relationship failed!

So, in summary, to some extent we are all motivated to date the same person over and over again in different disguises. However, if these relationships are not working for you, it will be necessary to change your "man program" so that you are attracting a different type of man into your life. And the only way to do that is through a process of awareness and evolution. Tomorrow (after you have completed the above exercise), try dating someone who does not quite conform to the pattern in your heart. He might feel strange, but he might also be a bit more of a success than your previous twelve boyfriends. And the next time, try dating someone even more different, and so on. Eventually, you will learn to recognize the aspects of a man which feel familiar at first, but which simply don't work for you in the long run.

✑ Law of the Jungle ✑
The definition of frustration is doing the same thing over and over again, each time anticipating a different result.

AMBIVALENCE

There are two sides to everything. You land a fantastic job and promotion, but you have to take on more responsibility and work longer hours. You are accepted into a prestigious college, but you'll have to work harder than you ever have in your life just to keep up with the other students. You meet a terrific man who wants to date you, but he might leave and break your heart. This man makes you really hot and you want to have sex with him, but you are not as experienced as you think you should be and are afraid to embarrass yourself. Very rarely do we encounter something or someone with no risk or downside. For some women, the ambivalence they feel about grabbing onto a good thing seems to paralyze them. This is especially true of women in the Elusive Love group discussed in Chapter 4.

We have been talking about unconscious programs, so by now it should come as no surprise that people are not generally aware of what they feel or want. They might *say* that they want to be in a relationship more than anything else in their life, but they don't *act* like they do.

Laurie's Story

Laurie is 40. She's a vice president at a major national corporation and, by her own admission, is consumed by her job. Laurie has never been married and it's been five years since her last relationship. Laurie says she is desperate to have a child. She's even considering having a child on her own. Laurie says that finding a relationship is an absolute priority for her. Sometimes it takes Gloria over two weeks to contact Laurie to tell her about a man she'd like to introduce her to. Laurie is so busy at work that she doesn't have time to return phone calls. Gloria will set up a time to talk at 8:00 or 9:00 in the evening, and Laurie doesn't call when she says she's going to, or she isn't at home when Gloria calls her at the appointed time. Laurie also won't meet a man who is over 45 years old. In an effort to light a bit of a fire under her, Gloria has explained to Laurie on several occasions that men who want children generally do not want to meet a woman who is over 38 years old, but to no avail. In addition to all of this, Laurie only wants to meet men who earn over a quarter of a million dollars a year. How desperate is Laurie to have a relationship and a child?

Miraculously, a man presented himself who would have been an excellent introduction for Laurie. He was very successful, a Harvard MBA, a great guy with a great personality, they shared similar interests and activities, and he very much wanted to have children. It took Laurie several days to get back to Gloria. When Gloria told her about him, she needed to think about it because he was 49. She really wasn't comfortable with his age. She took too long to think about it, and in that time he met someone else. The opportunity (and the risk) were gone.

. . . .

When it comes to relationships, there are many things to feel ambivalent about! Let's face it, relationships are hard work. It's no wonder if you're feeling that it's too much trouble and you just won't bother. Unfortunately, that ambivalence too often results in sabotage. You'll never get a chance to find out if you made the wrong decision because that decision will be made for you when you sabotage your chance.

The key to getting over your ambivalence is the same as above: Know yourself! Ask yourself what it is that you're afraid of. To help you with figuring out your fears, try the following.

EXERCISE

1. Write down your mother's name on a piece of paper, and then list all the things she got out of her relationship with your father. Then, make another list of what these things cost her. For example, maybe she got security, children, financial wealth, or status in the community. And maybe this cost her her independence, limited her to one man, and made her have sex which she didn't enjoy (come on, we all know whether or not our mothers enjoyed sex).

2. Write down what you learned about relationships from watching your parents interact. Was it that men are uncontrollable, that sex was awful, that women cry a lot, that there is a lot of yelling, or even that relationships don't last and your heart gets broken? Maybe it was exactly the opposite: that marriage is security, that your dad was perfect, that soulmates are worth waiting for. And maybe you won't be able to live up to this ideal, or feel that you don't deserve it. That would also be an excellent basis for sabotaging yourself.

Now, looking at these lists, figure out what you're afraid of. You might be afraid of failing, or you may be afraid of succeeding, but either way, you cannot address this fear unless you know what it is. Nobody is going to force you into a relationship that you don't want. Many women are perfectly happy living on their own without a man in their lives. Nobody says that you HAVE to be part of a couple. Like everything else, there are advantages as well as disadvantages to being in a relationship. But if a life without a man in it does not appeal to you, then you really have to do some major introspection to understand yourself.

DATING HORROR STORIES

Ask yourself the following question: Do I deserve to have a wonderful, caring, loving man in my life? The answer to this question is not as obvious as it may appear. If you are sabotaging yourself, then the answer is NO, by definition. If you deserved it, you wouldn't be sabotaging yourself now, would you? How can you tell if you are sabotaging yourself? Here are some dating horror stories. If any of these sound like something you might have done, then you need to stop it right away and make some major changes.

Sarah's Story

Sarah is 53 years old and is a member of our Elusive Love group. Sarah has had two boyfriends in her life. Each relationship lasted only a year or less. Sarah keeps saying she really feels like she's *now* ready for love in her life. About a year ago Sarah met a man whom she really liked; they had lots of things in common, and they seemed to click. The only problem was that Rick lived in a city about fifteen hundred miles away. They spoke on the phone often and talked about getting together again. After a couple of months of lengthy weekly phone conversations, Rick called Sarah and said he'd like to come see her the following weekend (about a week away). Sarah said that wouldn't work for her, but never gave Rick a reason why. The fact was that Sarah didn't have anything going on that weekend. There was no good reason why Rick couldn't come see her. She just felt that Rick should have given her more notice, that he shouldn't have just popped this on her at the last minute. Of course Sarah never suggested another time when Rick might have come to see her.

After that, Rick didn't call again in his usual three or four days. When one of Sarah's girlfriends pointed out to her that Rick probably felt rejected, and suggested to Sarah that maybe she should phone Rick, Sarah refused. Sarah felt very strongly that she wanted to be with a man who really wanted her and had to "work" for her.

Not long after that the phone calls stopped altogether. Sarah was successful in sabotaging any chance of a relationship with Rick. Sarah is excellent at making sure the hurdles a man has to jump are so high that he'll never be able to clear them.

Alison's Story

Alison is a single mom, who, because of her ticking clock, decided to have a child on her own. A year and a half ago she quit her job, uprooted herself and her one-year-old son, and moved to a city over a thousand miles from where she had been living to start a new life. Alison didn't know anyone in her new city. She knew she really wanted a relationship with a man. She decided, because of her situation, that she could use a little extra help, so she got in touch with Perfect Partners. Alison had a lot going for her. She is outgoing, bubbly, vivacious, and quite attractive. We had a great guy for her! Greg is a dad and loves kids, so he was totally open to meeting a single mom. They had lots in common. Greg and Alison had a little difficulty setting up a time to get together because of their schedules. Finally they connected, and Alison told Greg that she could meet him on her way home from some event she had to attend. Great! Until Alison, who has a full-time nanny, showed up for her date with Greg with her two-year-old son in tow! As if that weren't bad enough, Alison's son ran around the coffee shop, screamed, and threw a temper tantrum as only a two-year-old can, while Alison ignored him and acted like nothing out of the ordinary was happening. What was Alison thinking? Who would bring their young child on a "date," especially the first time they are going to meet someone?

After several more introductions and bits and pieces of unusual feedback from men after first meetings, we discovered that Alison was miserably unhappy. She was still very much in love with the father of her son and still hoping that he would leave his wife for her. Ahhhh... Waiting for the married man! How many otherwise incredibly intelligent women have done this? And they try to convince themselves they've moved on and are really serious about finding a "real" relationship by paying to join a dating service.

....

Jeff's Story

Jeff is an extremely successful 59-year-old businessman with an MBA and lots of worldwide business experience. Jeff's marriage of almost thirty years ended just over a year ago. His wife told him one day when he came home from work that it was over and she wanted him to move out. Jeff was stunned. Nevertheless, Jeff moved into a condominium on his own for about a year. He really missed having a relationship in his life and was serious about finding a wonderful woman.

Unfortunately, Jeff did nothing except talk about his ex-wife, all the things they did together, all the places they traveled to, and all of the gory details of the demise of their marriage, during every date. He even told one woman that he had called his wife just three days before to see if she wanted to get back together again. When Jeff's "date" showed surprise (we would say horror) that he was sitting there on a date with her, telling her he just called his wife to see if she would get back together with him, he said "Oh, I was really just calling my wife to see how she would react. I knew she wouldn't want to get back together."

Jeff was really very smitten with two women to whom he was introduced and couldn't figure out why they wouldn't go out with him again. When we gave Jeff some feedback on how his constant talking about his ex-wife on his first dates was making the women run screaming in the opposite direction, Jeff said he thought he was just being truthful. He felt he needed to let the women know what happened and how the marriage ended; he just didn't want to be hiding anything.

....

✑ LAW OF THE JUNGLE ✑
Too much information is a bad thing on a first date.

Theresa's Story

Theresa is a 39-year-old woman who has never been married, never lived with anyone, and desperately wants to have a family. She's bright, has a good career, and she's five-foot ten, so she wants to meet a man who is six feet tall or taller. Theresa also wants to meet a man who shares her religious background. Theresa was introduced to a highly eligible bachelor, who owned a very nice home in an excellent area of the city. Jim is 43, he's six-foot three, very good-looking, definitely wants a family, and he shares Theresa's religious background. In addition to this, they have lots of interests in common. BINGO!!! Theresa and Jim met for drinks one evening after work. Theresa really, really liked Jim. Everything about him was perfect. She really thought she would hear back from him. They had a nice evening. Jim agreed that they had a nice meeting and Theresa was bright and obviously had a good career, but Jim wasn't at all interested in seeing her again. It turns out that Theresa had three or more glasses of wine and got a little sloppy. Jim wasn't the least bit impressed. He felt that if someone couldn't control her drinking in a situation where she's trying to make a good first impression, what else would they not make good judgement calls about? Would she not be able to control her spending, her temper, or her eating? Theresa blew it! You only get one chance to make a good first impression. If finding a partner and having a family is so important to you, surely you can exercise restraint for an hour and a half.

. . . .

Chapter 7
Where to Find Men

It's a brave new dating world out there. If you haven't ventured out yet, take a deep breath and brace yourself. The good news is, there are lots of options and possibilities. The bad news is, this doesn't really make it a whole lot easier.

Dating is not for the faint of heart. This is a full-body contact sport. If you're not prepared to get knocked down and pick yourself back up, think again.

One of the biggest challenges facing 40-plus singles dating today is the whole idea of "blind" dating. Many of us met our former husband or partner when we were still in school or shortly thereafter, when there were still lots of single guys all about our own age and we were all hanging out together. You probably met a guy in one of your classes or through friends. You kind of liked him, and you thought maybe he liked you. You started flirting with him and he responded. There was a whole dance of flirting back and forth so that by the time he finally asked you out, he was pretty sure you'd say yes. You both knew by the first date that there was mutual interest.

It just happened! You didn't have to go looking for a boyfriend or make any special effort to find him. He was right there the whole time. So many of the women we talk to say they hate the idea of having to look for men. After all, they never had to do it before, thirty years ago when they last dated! They feel it's too contrived, too unnatural. Men should be out hunting for women, not the other way around. They don't want to make any special effort to find men. They will just meet them when the time is right. Somehow they will be found.

As much as we would like it to just happen "naturally," we'd like the knight in shining armor to ride up to our front door on his white horse, it's highly unlikely that he will do so. Even Cinderella had to dress herself up and go to the ball before she could meet Prince Charming. So, the statistics being what they are, you have to get out there and put yourself in their way.

John T. Molloy, in his thought-provoking book *Why Men Marry Some Women And Not Others*, provides some interesting insights from a long-term research project on single and engaged couples. He concludes that having an active social life and putting yourself in places where you are likely to meet single men are very important if you are looking to be in a relationship. Furthermore, women who go out at least two nights per week are *three times* more likely to marry than those who stay home, and going out three nights a week increases your chances even more. Three times appears to be the magic number to maximize your chances of meeting somebody.[20]

The status quo has changed in another big way. Nowadays, *everything is backwards* from what it used to be with regard to the way people decide on whether or not there is mutual attraction. When we were younger, we very often had the opportunity to get to know someone first, as a friend of a friend, classmate, etc., and then, as we got to know the person, the attraction grew. Unfortunately, with dating today, we seem to be looking for that magic attraction *first*, then we get to know someone if and only if that attraction is there. They never have a chance to grow on us. We respond only

20   Molloy, John T., *Why Men Marry Some Women And Not Others*, Warner Books, New York, 2003 pg. 149.

to our first impression of "attracted - not attracted." The danger here is that our unconscious mind immediately adopts this belief and we don't get a chance to replace it with a new belief based on experience with the other person, because there is no experience. We have already moved on. This is definitely backwards.

It's sad that so many people say "I just know in the first thirty seconds if there's anything there." The fact is it's impossible to know anything in the first thirty seconds except a knee-jerk reaction, which is NOT a reliable indicator of the possibility of a lasting relationship. We've had many situations where one of the two people, either the man or the woman, has said they weren't interested in seeing the other person again after the first meeting. And now, guess what? Those very same two people are either married or have been together for several years!

Sheila's Story

Sheila was a 39-year-old professional woman who had never been married, but who very much wanted to be married and have children. After she met the first man to whom she was introduced, she phoned to say that he was nice, but she wasn't interested in him. Both Sheila and Jack are fairly introverted, and you can imagine how awkward that first meeting might be with two nervous introverts. We had received feedback from Jack and knew he was very interested in Sheila. After much cajoling, we finally talked Sheila into seeing Jack again. Seven weeks later they were blissfully engaged, about seven months after that they were married, and about a year after that they had their first child. Now they have their second child, and are incredibly happy together.

. . . .

You see, Sheila was basing her decision to not date Jack again on her own initial reaction to a blind "date." Her judgment about him was off. She was admittedly very nervous about her first meeting with him. He was also not 100 percent himself at this first meeting. How can you possibly make any accurate assessments or decisions about an entire person and their life based on a meeting of an hour or so when nerves are on edge, emotions are high, and intelligence is low? Sheila would have totally missed a wonderful relationship with her soulmate, and two fantastic children, if she had stuck with her original decision not to see Jack again. What a terrible mistake she would have made.

✥ LAW OF THE JUNGLE ✥

When emotions are high, intelligence is low. Do NOT make potentially life-altering decisions when you're at your lowest point of intelligence.

This email came in to us from Rob, a client of Perfect Partners, just as we were writing this. We'd introduced Rob to Beth.

"I met with Beth today. We spent over two hours chatting; seemed to get on well.

As I escorted her to her car I asked her if we should see each other again-she replied that it is not worth it as there was no love at first sight for her. (She did say that maybe we could have dinner or something just as friends).

Was I hurt? A bit. But what a waste of time...my sense is that if she is looking for love at first sight she is very unrealistic - did you know that she was looking for that?"

. . . .

Some women seem to think that all men make decisions based on the first thirty seconds of meeting a woman. As you can see, this is not something that's exclusive to men. In fact, we don't see any gender bias on this. Plenty of women are just like Sheila and Beth. We can't urge you strongly enough not to make a decision about whether or not there is any chemistry based on meeting someone one time. We're quite certain that our success rate would be substantially higher if we could get all of our couples to see each other at least three times before making any decisions about the possible future of a relationship. This is one of the biggest challenges with dating today.

Interestingly, this is not just our finding. John Molloy found the same thing in his research. He reported in his book that his researchers "were astounded at the percentage of women who disliked the man they were marrying when they had first met. They were also surprised by how often these relationships worked out."[21] Molloy, in really trying to help women understand how they can be more successful in finding a partner, goes on to tell women that if you didn't click with someone the first time you met him there is a high chance, based on what he's found in statistically valid research, that you might connect on the second time. In his words, "don't be afraid to give a guy a second chance – it just might improve your chances."[22]

Gloria's Mother's Story

I can remember my mother telling me about how she couldn't stand my father when she first met him. Her father had brought my father, who worked at the same company as my grandfather, home after work to play cards one evening. My mother thought he was obnoxious and very unattractive. My father asked her out and she refused him. But my grandfather kept bringing him home after work to play cards. And my father kept asking my mother out. Eventually my mother relented, but only because she wanted someone to go to a dance with. She still didn't like him one bit! Needless to say, my mother changed her mind. They were incredibly happily married for over fifty years.

. . . .

. . . .

21   Ibid pg. 73

22   Ibid pg. 73

The fact is it's been scientifically proven that familiarity breeds *content*. In 1967, a class on speech persuasion at Oregon State University was shocked to find a mysterious student attending the lectures. This student was wrapped in a big black bag from head to foot, with only his bare feet protruding under the bag. He came to class for two months, during which time he said nothing and did not identify himself. The professor knew who he was, but no one else did. At first, the students reacted with hostility. At the end of two months, however, their hostility had turned to curiosity and then to friendship.[23]

In another experiment, a group of students were shown photos of senior graduating men from Michigan State University. Each photograph was presented a different number of times for two seconds. Then subjects were asked how much they might like the man in each photograph. Overall, for the majority of pictures, the higher the frequency of exposure, the higher the rating on liking.[24]

What do these two experiments mean? They imply that mere exposure to somebody, even when no relationship exists, is enough to make others like them more. In other words, if you see someone over and over again, your liking and comfort around them increases. You begin to find them attractive and likable. Maybe you didn't swoon over that man you saw yesterday on a blind date, but give him time and he might just start to look good to you. That's how humans, as well as other animals, are programmed. The immediate reaction to something new and strange may be negative, but with repeated exposure, people and things grow on us.

☙ LAW OF THE JUNGLE ❧
Familiarity breeds content.

23   Robert B. Zajonc, "Attitudinal effects of mere exposure," in Samuel Himmelfarb and Alice H. Eagly *Readings in Attitude Change*, John Wiley and Sons, 1974 page 52.

24   Ibid, page 73-74.

So, how do you even find a man with whom to go out on a "date" in the first place? We wish we had some absolutely earth-shattering revelations to share with you here, but we don't. There are lots of ways in which you can potentially meet men today. We highly recommend you do as many of them as you can, to increase your opportunity of finding Mr. Right. You will most likely have to move out of your comfort zone to get what you're looking for. And, yes, this will take some work. Mr. Right is not likely to fall into your lap. You know the old saying "If you always do what you've always done, you'll always get what you've always gotten. In order to get what you've never gotten, you've got to do what you've never done." You're going to have to force yourself to get out of your comfort zone and do new things. If you're not willing to do this, don't be surprised when you get the same results you've had to date: NOTHING.

Here are the major options on where to meet men.

The "Natural" Ways

Your Personal Network - Friends, Acquaintances and Relatives

Cost: FREE

Quantity/Availability of Men: Usually pretty slim

Quality of Men: Broad range

Security/Personal Comfort Level: HIGH

If you're serious about finding a partner you should definitely be using your personal network of friends, family members, co-workers, neighbors, and just about anyone else you know. This means more than just moaning to your best girlfriend about how difficult it is to meet men. In order for this to be effective, you need to be able to actually talk to your friends, relatives, neighbors, and associates about the fact that you're actively looking for someone and ask them to be on the lookout for you. The more you talk to people about the types of things you like to do, your hobbies, activities, and interests, the more likely it is that someone will come to mind that they hadn't thought of before as a possible match for you.

The biggest downside of this source is that it can be tricky to tell a friend that their husband's cousin's wife's brother isn't exactly your cup of tea. Sometimes friends, with all of the best intentions in the world, will introduce you to men who make you come away scratching your head saying, "What were they thinking? What on earth did they think we'd have in common?" Usually to this your friend will say something like, "But he's such a nice guy."

Obviously, if everyone could just rely on their personal network to help them find Mr. Right, there wouldn't be a need for a dating industry that's over half a billion dollars a year. John T. Molloy (2003) reports that, in his long-term research study on engaged couples, a majority of engaged women over 40 thought that the best way to meet potential mates was through friends, and at least 64 percent of the dates that women over 40 had were with men whom they met in this way. However, fewer than one-third of marriages resulted from these setups.[25] So don't be too disappointed if you need to do more than count on your friends to find a partner.

The Workplace

Cost: FREE

Quantity/Availability of Men: Very dependent on the type of work you do and the work environment

Quality of Men: Fairly High

Security/Personal Comfort Level: HIGH

For many people today the workplace is off limits as a source of meeting single men. Many companies have personnel policies that prohibit or strongly discourage dating fellow employees. Even if the company doesn't have this policy, lots of singles agree

. . . .

25   Ibid pg. 141-142.

that it can be pretty tricky to date someone in the office, at least someone who works in the same department or in an area that you interact with frequently within the office. What do you do if the relationship goes sour? It can create a very awkward and uncomfortable situation if you have to continue to deal with your ex-beau on a day-to-day basis. Of course if either person is in any type of management position, and the other person works for them, this just compounds the complexities of a potential relationship.

Today, large numbers of people work in small businesses with ten or fewer employees. These people often say that the only new people they meet are clients or suppliers. Again, most people would say you just can't date a client. In fact, in some industries, such as the legal profession, there are potential conflicts of interest, and it's illegal for a lawyer to have a relationship with a client.

Unfortunately, the top three sources through which we used to meet people when we were in our twenties are just not there for the 40-plus dater. We're out of school so we're not meeting a whole variety of new guys in classes. We're not hanging out with a group of co-ed single friends, who all have more co-ed single friends that we can potentially meet. And we're no longer in a work environment where we can freely date lots of single guys. So again, the ways that we used to consider to be the "natural" ways of meeting people have all but evaporated. We're left with what many women feel are the *"unnatural"* ways of meeting men. "I can't believe I have to pay to find a man" many women tell us. These relatively new "manufactured" ways of meeting people are quickly becoming the new dating norm. Unfortunately, these new methods have created unnatural and backwards behaviors.

Here are your "manufactured" men-meeting options.

The "Unnatural" Ways

Singles Events

Cost: $ - $$

Quantity/Availability of Men: Usually significantly fewer men than women

Quality of Men: Below average - average

Security/Personal Comfort Level: MEDIUM

There are a broad range of singles events available today. These include things like singles dances; hiking groups; golfing events; skiing clubs; volleyball, softball, and basketball leagues; wine tastings; museum, symphony, or opera groups; and travel groups. Some activities, like golfing events and softball and basketball leagues will draw more men, but generally speaking, men aren't joiners. Men socialize differently than women do. With the exception of team sports, men don't tend to do things in groups. When was the last time you saw a group of guys getting together to go to dinner and the theater? It just doesn't happen. With most of these activities there are far fewer men than there are women. The men who do go to singles events tend to be a little lower on the socio-economic scale, in our opinion.

Having said this, if you're interested in a specific activity, and chances are you're going to be doing it anyway, why not join a singles group that does this? Or if you're interested in taking up a new activity, again, why not join a singles group? In a worst-case scenario, you'll enjoy the activity and meet some interesting women. And you may just meet a wonderful man.

Dinner Events

Cost: $$ - $$$

Quantity/Availability of Men: Average

Quality of Men: Average – Average +

Security/Personal Comfort Level: MEDIUM

Most good dinner-dating companies make sure there are equal numbers of men and women at any dinner. Typically there would be six to ten people at a dinner. If you're looking at joining one of these services, make sure they make this guarantee. Also, see if they have age-appropriate groups. You don't want to be stuck with men that are way too old or way too young for you. We also recommend that you check about a pay-per-dinner service, so that you can evaluate the quality of the men that come to the dinners. Ask if the company does any type of screening or interview with the dinner guests. What criteria do they use for choosing people for any given dinner party?

Speed Dating

Cost: $ - $$
Quantity/Availability of Men: Good
Quality of Men: Medium - Low
Security/Personal Comfort Level: LOW – MEDIUM/LOW

Speed dating is perhaps a slight step above online dating. There are equal numbers of men and women at the events, or very close. There's no screening done other than on age range. Similar to online dating, it's largely a visual medium. It's a game of who looks best in three to five minutes or so. It's all about first impressions and not much on substance. However, you do get to meet quite a few people in a short time frame at relatively low cost. Most speed dating groups skew younger and are targeting the under-40 crowd. Check carefully to see if any speed dating event you go to has age-appropriate men.

Dating Services

Cost: $$$ - $$$$
Quantity/Availability of Men: Low
Quality of Men: Broad range, tends to be higher
Security/Personal Comfort Level: MEDIUM HIGH

Dating services are the most expensive medium to use, but can result in a more secure and pleasant experience for you. A good service should have an extensive interview and screening process. With the exception of introductions from friends, this should be the source which would provide you with the highest level of security, personal comfort, privacy, and confidentiality.

Most services have significantly more women than men in their databases. You should ask this question and make sure you get a straightforward answer. Again, men are not joiners, so they tend not to join dating services. Also, as we've seen, the statistics favor the men, so they have less need for dating services. How does the service get the men? Does the service have men in the appropriate age range for you? Many services, but not all, have a challenge finding men for women who are 45-plus. Be sure you understand exactly how the service works. Many services do not use pictures. How much information do you find out about a possible introduction prior to meeting them? How is an introduction made? Does the man contact you, or do you have to contact him? Do you have the right to accept or decline an introduction without the introduction's "counting"? Is there a feedback process? How personalized is the service you're paying for? Does the person interviewing you do the matching, or is there a computerized matching department? How much information does the service have about you? Are you comfortable that they have a solid sense of who you are and what you're looking for?

With a truly good, highly personalized dating service, your chances of finding a great match are probably higher than they would be with any other type of service we've discussed. The price can range from $500 to $250,000 for these services.

Online Dating

Cost: $

Quantity/Availability of Men: High

Quality of Men: Broad range but tends to be lower
Security/Personal Comfort Level: LOW

Online dating started off in 1995 when Match.com was the first site to appear on scene. Since then the growth in online dating has been huge; it's now a half-billion-dollar a year industry. In addition to a number of mass market mainstream sites like Match.com, eHarmony.com, Yahoo! Personals, and LavaLife.com, there are all kinds of niche sites for people of specific ethnic and/or religious backgrounds, as well as sites like GolfMates.com, ConservativeMatch.com, LiberalHearts.com, EquestrianCupid.com, CowboyCowgirl.com, GothicMatch.com, OverweightSingles.com, USMilitarySingles.com, and on and on.

Online dating is obviously extremely popular and relatively inexpensive, though time-consuming. Its popularity is both a blessing and a curse. The good news is that there are millions of people in North America on online dating sites. In any twelve-month period approximately 45 million North Americans will give internet dating a try. So there are lots of possibilities, lots of people to choose from. The bad news is, because there are so many people to choose from, finding just the right person for you can be like finding a needle in a haystack. Anyone who has put a toe into the water of online dating knows it can literally take hours to wade through all of the profiles of prospective matches. It also can be extremely difficult to really determine much of anything about who a person is from an online profile. For this reason, many of the online sites are working hard to develop personality profiling tools to help fine-tune the search process. eHarmony was the first big site to launch in August 2000 with their 436-question personality survey. Now there's Chemistry.com launched by Match.com to compete with eHarmony, and PerfectMatch.com with their "Total Compatibility System."

Even personality profiling tools won't help with one of the very significant challenges of online dating: The problem of people's misrepresenting themselves. Unfortunately, it's way too common for people to lie about their ages, shave pounds off their weight, post pictures of themselves from years long gone by, and exaggerate their job title and/or income level. Online dating is a visual game. It's all about who's got the best picture posted. This is a sad commentary on just how superficial we've become in our society today. It also substantiates our earlier comments about dating today being a reverse process. First we find out if there's any attraction, then we get to know someone, rather than getting to know someone to see if there might be any attraction.

We were pleased to see that many of the ideas we've put forth in this book have been backed up in the fascinating book *Freakonomics* by Steven Levitt and Stephen Dubner. Steven Levitt is a well-known economist who has distilled the science of economics "to its most primal aim: explaining how people get what they want."[26] One of the many things they discuss is an analysis from data of over 20,000 active users of a mainstream online dating site. In this research, 56 percent of the users were men, and the age range of all users was 21 to 35. Levitt and Duber discuss the many ways in which people misrepresent themselves in the world of online dating. Some people said they were richer, taller, skinnier, or better-looking than average. It appears that three out of four big earners were exaggerating about how much money they made. People tended to add an inch onto their height, and women said they weighed about twenty pounds less than the national average. Interestingly, 72 percent of women and 68 percent of men said they were "above average" in looks. Levitt and Dubner conclude that "the typical online dater is either a fabulist, a narcissist, or simply resistant to the meaning of 'average'. (Or perhaps they are

. . . .

26   Levitt, Steven D. and Dubner, Stephen J., *Freakonomics*, HarperCollins Publishers, New York, 2006 pg. x

all just pragmatists...)"[27] Unless you say these wonderful things about yourself, no one will even bother to look at your profile.

It's clear from the research that in order to be successful online you must post a photo. Men who don't have photos only get 60 percent as much email as men with photos. Women who don't have photos posted only get 24 percent as much email as their competition.

The preferences shown by online daters fit with what we said in Chapter 5—What Men Want. No surprises here. "For men, a woman's looks are of paramount importance. For women, a man's income is terribly important. The richer the man is the more e-mails he receives."[28] They also said that short men have a big disadvantage, which probably explains why so many men lie about their height. On the other hand, women lie about their weight because being overweight is deadly.

If it's any consolation, the authors of *Freakonomics* have shown that in all areas of life, business, politics, and personal relationships "the gulf between the information we publicly proclaim and the information we know to be true is often vast."[29]

It will be very interesting to see what the long-term impact of online dating is on society. Clearly our societal need for instant gratification has now moved into the dating realm, with literally millions of people the world over at your fingertips at any given moment. If you get dumped, or dump someone, you can find someone else within seconds. But of even greater concern is the addictive "shopaholic" nature of internet dating. There's a buzz, a bit of a high, from the next "smile," "wink," or email you might get from a new potential match. It's like an endless candy shop with unlimited flavors. And maybe the next one will be even tastier than the last one. At some point we'll have to mature and realize relationships

. . . .

27   Ibid pg. 75
28   Ibid pg. 76
29   Ibid pg. 77

are not all about the buzz and romance. In order to have any kind of endurance and meaning, a relationship has to go way beyond the initial hormone-flying stage. But we've heard from way too many people that this online dating thing can be addictive, and frankly, it makes a lot of sense to us how this can be. Will we start having to institute new twelve-step Daters Anonymous programs? What a scary thought.

Despite everything we've just said, we are NOT trying to dissuade you from trying online dating. It is definitely the biggest, most popular option available today. We just want you to go into it with your eyes wide open. We suggest you check out a variety of sites. You should look at some of the larger mainstream sites, as well as several niche sites, if there are some that fit a particular interest of yours. We suggest using sites that give you more information on education, career, and income. You may want to try out one of the sites that use some type of personality profiling. At least with these sites you'll know that the other person has put some time and effort into going through the survey to get their profile online. We don't suggest you spend hours and hours emailing people back and forth, then talking on the phone for weeks before meeting. We suggest that when you've found a profile that interests you, you have relatively brief email and telephone interactions with the purpose of trying to set up an opportunity to meet for coffee or drinks in a public place. Generally, we suggest being short, sweet and to-the-point in these "transactions."

✑ LAW OF THE JUNGLE ✑

If you truly want to increase your chances of finding Mr. Right try as many of these sources as you possibly can.

Cathy Thorne © www.everydaypeoplecartoons.com

THE PROBLEM WITH PLAYING GAMES IS THAT IT ATTRACTS THE KIND OF GUY WHO LIKES TO PLAY GAMES.

Chapter 8

The Big Date and Beyond

It is one of those little ironies of life that people in this society try to learn about a potential mate's true and sincere character from a completely artificial situation. We are referring to The Date. People who go on a date are torn in two opposite directions: The desire to get to know the other person and be known in return, versus the inclination to put their best foot forward in order to impress and be accepted. When both parties are doing this, you can imagine that it becomes a most inefficient process for judging character. In our opinion, women are much better off when there is somebody out there to vouch for their date's potential, such as a mutual friend or work associate or even a matchmaker. However, for those of you flying solo, and especially for those who are doing internet dating, it's all you've got.

There is a whole culture around The Date, with very strict etiquette. At least, there is as far as women are concerned. Women tell us that many men seem to be blissfully unaware of what the rules of The Date are, and must be unceremoniously educated on the matter. Interviews with men indicate that this is in fact the case. Men do understand that there are some basic rules, but do not have the long laundry list of tests and criteria that women seem to carry.

In terms of evolutionary psychology, this makes a lot of sense. The outcome of mating could have adverse consequences for a woman.[30] If the man left after sex and refused to make a parental investment, she could find herself in very bad circumstances indeed. How could she be sure that he was going to stick around? The only way was to be totally skeptical about his motives until he proved himself through perseverance and devotion. Too much trust and she could find herself alone. Too much skepticism and she would make it impossible for the man to prove himself. It's a fine line that women still walk today.

Today's modern women have designed an obstacle course for their suitors in order to test their worthiness. The test is given during The Date. We call it the Prince Charming Test. By setting up The Date as an examination, women are ensuring that they will discover how much the man knows about the rules of The Date, but it is not a good test for judging the man's character or abilities. Only observation in real-life circumstances will give you that. See if you can identify with the seven deadly sins of dating.

· · · · · · · · · · · ·

30   see discussion in: Rebhahn, Peter, "Mixed signals – research on gender differences in interpreting sexual signals," "Pyschology Today," July 2000.

In Search of Prince Charming

Women over 40 are still looking for Prince Charming! It seems that they still have a fairytale ideal of the man of their dreams and that "oh-so-incredible" romantic date. Women still want to be swept off their feet. It's apparent that women have pretty tough expectations of men. They've set the bar fairly high. Heaven help the man who doesn't pass the Prince Charming Test!

We often hear women say that they just want a man to take them on a "real date." Many women feel like they haven't been on a real date in years. What on earth is this elusive "real date"? What are women looking for? Well, not too much, really. There are seven things that a man needs to do to pass the Prince Charming Test. If he doesn't successfully complete any of these criteria he's committed a dating sin.

The seven deadly dating sins of men are:

Sin #1 – The sin of indecision and wimpiness. If a man can't choose a restaurant to take you to, he's a loser.

Sin #2 – The sin of ungentlemanly conduct. If the man doesn't open doors for you and pull out your chair for you, he's definitely not a gentleman, and your mother just wouldn't approve.

Sin #3 – The fashion sin. If the man isn't dressed nicely—neat, clean, fashionably and appropriately attired—he's toast.

Sin #4 – The sin of bad table manners. If a man has poor table manners, doesn't know what fork to use or how to hold it, you'll never be able to take him home for Thanksgiving dinner, so ditch him now.

Sin #5 – The sin of being cheap. If a man doesn't pay for the coffee, drinks, or a meal, he's cheap. Run as fast as you can.

Sin #6 — The sin of the lost chariot. If the man doesn't come pick you up at your door in a nice clean car and whisk you off to your dream date, he's not worth it.

Sin #7 — The sin of lack of perseverance. If a man doesn't jump through hoops for you, don't lower your standards; he's not deserving of you!

Women are generally looking for these things in a man from the first time they meet him. He's got to pass the test right away. The more insecure the woman, the more exacting the test. Now, some of these sins seem pretty sensible. Who wants to be with a guy who is not generous, or who can't make a decision to save his life? Who wants to be stuck with a guy who was raised by wolves and doesn't have the least idea of how to treat a woman, eat in a restaurant, or who dresses like a slob? Holy Prince Alarming! What we are suggesting, however, is that instead of a knee-jerk Pass-Fail, you try to understand the context of their behavior before you make a decision to reject them.

◯ LAW OF THE JUNGLE ◯

The Prince Charming Test is good for discovering whether the guy knows the rules of dating, but it is not a good way to discover a man's true character.

Here's the problem. Men have a very different take on this whole dating thing. If a man is meeting a woman one-on-one for the first time, whether it's through internet dating, speed dating, a dating service, or a set-up through friends, this is usually NOT a date in his mind. Most men do not look at this first meeting as a "date." To the man, it is strictly a meeting. He doesn't know you. He's *meeting* you to see if he's interested in asking you out on a *date*. Because this is just a meeting, he's not in "date mode," and is likely to fail the Prince Charming Test because of a misunderstanding. Since this isn't a date, he's not thinking about all of those romantic, chivalrous gestures, and he may not even be thinking about picking up the tab. This does NOT mean that he has no manners and should be written off as a lost cause. It's very possible he's entirely different when he's in date mode. For some men, it may take them three or four "meetings" with you before they kick into date mode.

Arlene's Story

Arlene was recently out on her second "date" with Nathan. Nathan is a highly intelligent, highly analytical, very well-mannered multi-millionaire. Nathan took Arlene out to a very nice restaurant for lunch for their first "date." Now they were at one of the nicest restaurants in the city for dinner. Arlene likes Nathan and thinks he's very gracious and interesting, and worth spending some time with to see if things will go anywhere, but she's not feeling anything. At some point during the dinner Arlene decided she was going to go out on a limb a bit, and she said something about "by the time you're on a second date..." Nathan was very surprised and responded in all sincerity with "Is this a date?" To which Arlene, in total amazement, said "Yes, Nathan. Man, woman, restaurant, wine, dinner... date!"

. . . .

So even when it seems to you like it's a date, sometimes you just can't tell. Or can you? Trust us, you'll know for sure when *he* knows for sure.

Gloria's Story

Eric is the very first man I met when I started my dating service. He came referred to me by some friends of mine. When I met Eric he started flirting with me in a very mild and understated manner, but at the time, I was dating someone else. Also, this was my business. I needed to be professional, I couldn't go dating every man I met and then tell other women "I didn't like him, but you'll love him." But we got to know each other as friends because we played golf together four or five times over the summer. We didn't see each other again until we met at a Christmas party. Shortly after the Christmas party, Eric asked me if I wanted to get together for a "catch-up" dinner between Christmas and New Year. This turned out to be a dinner party with three other couples, at our mutual friends' house. He met me at my place in a cab and I drove us to our friends. After dinner I dropped him off at the curb in front of his condo and he never said anything about getting together. I wasn't sure if this was a "date" or not.

Much to my surprise, three days later in the middle of the afternoon on New Year's Eve, Eric phoned to see if I was still free that night. He invited me down to his place; he was going to cook us dinner. (Friends at the dinner party had asked everyone what they were doing on New Year's Eve. It just so happened that neither Eric nor I had any plans.) When I arrived at his condo, I was very impressed: the lights were dim, candles were lit, and he obviously had music planned out for the evening. We had a nice dinner, but when I left at about 1:00 A.M. I was really confused. He walked me all of about fifteen feet to the door of his condo and said goodbye. That was it!! He never offered to walk me the block or so to the parking garage where my car was parked three levels down. He never made any attempt to kiss me, and the conversation during the evening was like I was one of the guys. What about the candles and the music? I remember telling one of my girlfriends the next day that I had a nice time, but the guy never even offered to walk me to my car at one o'clock in the morning! I wasn't impressed, but I left a voicemail message at his office on New Year's Day thanking him for dinner.

By now I was pretty stumped. This didn't seem like a man who would waste his time with someone if he wasn't interested. I decided I would return the dinner by inviting Eric to my place for dinner the following weekend. I pulled out all the stops, cooked up a storm, and really tried hard to impress him. I also tried to flirt with him. I'm quite a natural flirt, but I just couldn't get anywhere. When he left that night I didn't feel like I'd made any progress at moving this relationship along. By the end of the day Monday I still hadn't received a phone call or an email thanking me for the dinner. I was baffled and *again* unimpressed with him.

It was driving me crazy, so I decided to take the initiative to send him a flirtatious email. We exchanged a series of emails and by Wednesday, Eric invited me out to dinner at one of the best restaurants in the city for Saturday evening. This time, Eric picked me up in his car, he opened doors for me, he pulled out my chair, he took my hand, he kissed me, he was very romantic. It was a fairytale date and the toad had turned into Prince Charming! We've been together ever since. To this day, Eric says the first three dinners were *not* dates; they were merely dinners with an interesting person who happened to be a female. Go figure! The fact is, when he finally decided it was our first "official" date it was totally obvious and he did everything right.

. . . .

So, if you really want to see how the guy performs on The Date, your job is to get the man into date mode. He's got to be interested enough in you to want to officially take you out on a date. Until then, you need to work your charm and be patient, maybe more so than you ever thought you could be, and reserve judgement.

⤜ LAW OF THE JUNGLE ⤐

Sometimes, what appears to be a date to you is not a date to him. Before you evaluate him, make sure he is in date mode.

MEETING GUIDELINES FOR WOMEN

Regardless of the superficiality of The Date, it is just as well to learn the etiquette and rules surrounding it so that it comes naturally to you. If you don't have to think about it and wonder whether or not you're making a *faux pas*, you are much more likely to present yourself as relaxed and comfortable, have a better time, and make a better impression. We have provided some modern rules of dating for you. As you will see, some of them are directly related to the seven deadly sins that men make.

First, let's start with The Meeting, a preamble to The Date. Again, this is where the two of you meet to see if there's any interest in going on a date together. A lot of the rules which govern The Meeting are the same as for The Date.

1. The First Phone Call:

Assuming the man calls you, thank him for calling. Ask him a little bit about himself. The main purpose of this phone call is to set up a time and place to meet. Be flexible on where and when to meet and if his suggested locations don't work for you be prepared to offer an alternative. Ensure you each have your own transportation. Ask for his cell phone number in case you need to reach him just prior to your meeting, and be sure he has your cell phone number. Be prepared to tell him how to recognize you and ask how you'll recognize him. If you are really looking forward to meeting him, remember to let him know.

We highly recommend that you keep this first phone call relatively brief. Technology, like the telephone or email, is a buffer between people. It blurs a lot of information which you would normally get in a one-on-one meeting, and could lead to misunderstandings between people who are essentially strangers to each other. Some people are better at phone conversations than others. We've had too many experiences where one person drew completely incorrect conclusions about the other person from a phone conversation. So keep it short and sweet. This is not the time to tell him your life story.

2. The First Meeting:

We suggest that a first meeting be kept relatively casual. Usually people meet for coffee or drinks. The goal is to be comfortable and relaxed, and to take as much pressure off the situation as possible. If the conversation is going really well, it's always easier to extend the time you're going to spend together than it is to try to extract yourself from a longer dinner meeting.

Do not go into this first meeting with the intention of determining if this is the man you're going to spend the rest of your life with. In fact, don't allow yourself to go down that road at all. Approach this meeting as an opportunity to have fun and meet an interesting person. Play a game with yourself. Give yourself three goals to accomplish. One should be that you're going to come away from the meeting knowing what color his eyes are (this will ensure you make eye contact). Another goal might be that you're going to find out one thing he really likes to do in his spare time, and the third might be that you're going to find out where he grew up. Keep it simple and don't expect to feel any chemistry or attraction. This *does not* always happen right away.

3. How to Dress:

Men and women alike tell us how important a well-groomed and attractive appearance is at a first meeting. Refer to Chapter 5 to ensure you present yourself at your very best. The feedback we regularly get from men is that they really appreciate it when a woman has made an effort to look her best for their meeting.

Do not dress suggestively for this first meeting. If you have really long fingernails, cut them back. In fact, get yourself a manicure. If you have a choice between contact lenses and glasses, go for the contact lenses. Do not wear a lot of clunky jewellery, perfume, or heavy makeup.[31]

. . . .

31 Hogan, Kevin and William Horton, *Selling Yourself To Others – The New Psychology Of Sales,* Pelican Publishing Company, Gretna 2002.

4. Arrival and Seating:

Arrive on time. Be on the lookout for the man you're meeting so you recognize him. Smile and greet him. If you arrive early, ask for a table that allows you to sit so that you are facing most of the people in the room. This means that your date will have to give you his undivided attention and not be distracted by other people in the room. The best possible arrangement is for you to sit at a right angle to your date.[32]

5. What Not to Do When You're Seated

We know that you're probably nervous, but for heaven's sake, don't fidget and keep your hands and feet still! People who move around a lot give the impression of being uncomfortable, which in turn makes others uncomfortable. Legs that cross and uncross, and hands that play with your hair, neck, and face create the impression of being nervous. If you don't know what to do with your hands, just cup them together in your lap and keep them there when you're not eating.[33]

6. Eye Contact

Try to maintain eye contact for a few seconds at a time so that you are looking at your date's eyes about two-thirds of the time. While you're at it, have a look at the pupils of his eyes when he's talking. Are they big and black? If they are, it means that either the room is really dark, or that he likes what he sees (you). Needless to say, if you are wearing sunglasses, ditch them.[34]

7. Ordering:

Turn off any cell phones or pagers and give your date your undivided attention. If you're meeting for a drink, make sure you

. . . .

32   Ibid

33   Ibid

34   Ibid

keep your alcohol consumption to a minimum. It never leaves a positive impression to get a little sloppy.

8. Conversation:

Ask him about himself. Find out more about what he does for a living, what activities and hobbies he's involved in. If he has children, ask him about his children. Make eye contact and actively listen to what he is sharing with you. Strive for a balance in the conversation of his telling you a bit about his life, and your telling him about yours. Laugh at his jokes and nod your head when he says something you agree with.

DO NOT turn your meeting into a job interview. Don't plaster him with a million questions in an effort to learn as much as you possibly can about him so you can decide if you want to see him again. This should not be an oral examination.

DO NOT talk about your former spouse/partner/boyfriend(s). Many men and women have told us that they just feel they have to be honest and let the other person know what happened, why their marriage broke up. I don't know how many times we have to tell people not to talk about their ex. This topic should definitely be left for conversations when you know each other better and are pursuing a relationship. This is a real turnoff for a first meeting.

DO NOT talk about previous people you've met through your various dating experiences. This is a no-win situation. You may either have met too many people, or not enough. You run the risk of sounding like you're very picky and critical or you're comparing everyone, and the man has to "pass the test." Men do not like to be put in this situation. They do not like to be compared to other men.

The most frequent criticisms we get in our date feedback is that someone talked too much about their "ex," the other people they've met in their dating experience, or that they talked about themselves the whole time and didn't ask any questions about the other person, or the exact opposite of this, that it felt like a job interview because the person grilled them with a list of questions.

9. Ending the Meeting:

Ideally the meeting should last about an hour. When wrapping up the meeting, give a valid reason for your departure. Give him some positive feedback to end on a good note. For example, "It was a pleasure meeting you, I enjoyed our conversation, you've certainly had an interesting life," or "It sounds like things are going really well for you in your career." If you enjoyed meeting him and you'd like to stay in touch, we highly recommend exchanging business cards.

Since this is a meeting and not a date, you should be prepared to pay for yourself. If a man offers to pay the first time you're meeting, allow him to do so, and make sure you thank him. We do, however, recommend that you offer to pay for your own drinks. If the man pays for both of you, at least it's not a big expense at this stage.

10. Realistic Expectations:

After the first meeting, give it a chance to go somewhere. If you had a pleasant time and the conversation was enjoyable but you are not sure there was any spark, we *highly recommend* getting together one or two more times. Often people are uncomfortable during that first meeting and are not entirely themselves. Our experience shows that it is often on the second or third date that the spark happens because it takes time to get to know people. Several of our couples that are now married or in long-term relationships would not be together had we not strongly encouraged them to meet a second and third time.

Do not expect to feel instant chemistry. This process of "blind" dating is different and sometimes takes a little more patience. Often those relationships that start off with that instant spark flare up quickly with lots of physical attraction, but fizzle out just as quickly.

Email is a great way to communicate. If the first meeting went well and you'd like to stay in touch, email gives you an easy way to thank him for the first date. Tell him how much you enjoyed meeting him and let him know he can call you if he'd like to get together again.

We encourage you to be honest and straightforward with the men you meet. If, after the first meeting, you feel there was no connection on which to develop a relationship, you can send a brief email to say thank you and convey your honest intentions. A simple communication saying you just don't feel that special spark is sufficient. It's best to represent yourself truthfully throughout this process. It can end up reflecting badly on you if you make up stories to avoid hurting someone's feelings.

Regardless of whether the meeting was a success or not, if the man has paid for your drinks, it is common courtesy to send him an email or leave him a voice message to thank him.

What About Those Seven Deadly Sins of Dating?

Okay. You've met for coffee and decided that you like each other enough to go on The Date. This is where women's perceptions and men's motives can conflict. A lot of our advice is the same as in the first meeting. Here are some additional points.

11. How to Choose the Place:

It is easy for the man to fail the Prince Charming Test right off the bat if he doesn't manage to pick the right place for The Date. Women clearly state that they want the man to take the lead here. They want the man to have a plan for The Date. In order to pass the test, he should call with a restaurant he's chosen, or perhaps an option of two restaurants for you to choose from. We have heard women come right out and say "I make decisions all day long in my work, I take responsibility for everything. For once, I don't want to have to make any decisions. I don't want to have to take on more responsibility. Can't he at least do this?" Well, that doesn't sound too unreasonable, does it? In addition to this, it can be quite uncomfortable for a woman when a new date asks her where she'd like to go for dinner. If she chooses a modest restaurant that's fairly inexpensive, he might think she doesn't have much class or taste in food. If she chooses a place that's pricey or trendy, he might think she's quite presumptuous about spending his money.

However, when we asked men, they thought they were being the most thoughtful when they let the woman decide where she'd like to go for dinner. After all, the man doesn't even know yet what kind of food she likes. Remember, we're talking about a brand-new dating experience. If you've never met before, the man might not be familiar with your part of town to suggest anything convenient for you. Men are also aware that, unfortunately, women these days need to be concerned for their personal safety, and they want the woman to feel comfortable with her surroundings. So think again if you're feeling like the guy is a loser if he can't even choose a restaurant.

Donna's Story

Donna is a 43-year-old divorced working mother of two, with one heck of a busy schedule and lots of juggling going on in her life. Tom is a widower with sole custody of two young boys, a very successful business, and an equally busy schedule. It took Donna and Tom several weeks to coordinate a time to get together to meet. When Tom called to set up the meeting, Donna was angry and insulted that he hadn't decided where they were going to meet. She suggested that he call her back when he had an idea. Tom called her back later that day and suggested they meet at a very nice bar in an upscale hotel. That made Donna even angrier because she just doesn't meet men in hotels on first or second contacts. Donna gave Tom an alternative place and they met there. After all of that Donna didn't put much effort into getting ready for the meeting. She wore jeans and a T-shirt.

. . . .

Now, if Donna had such strong feelings about what would be an appropriate venue for a first meeting, wouldn't it have been much easier for her to suggest a place where she would have felt comfortable right from the very beginning? Poor Tom was damned no matter what he did.

12. Picking Up And Dropping Off:

This one is tricky. Most men will offer to meet you somewhere, and this is exactly what they should do. Unless you already know him fairly well, for your personal safety, you should be certain you're meeting him in a public place and you have your own transportation. You should not allow him to come pick you up. This would be something you would do only after you've gone out several times and you feel comfortable that you're not putting yourself in any danger by having him pick you up.

13. What To Order:

Your mother probably told you to order from the middle of the menu; not the most or least expensive thing but something in the middle. This is good advice, to which we would add: don't order anything that's hard to eat or else you run the risk of wearing it on your blouse, and don't order anything that you have to pick up with your hands.

14. Who Pays:

The protocol for who pays for what is different today. It's totally inappropriate for you to expect the man to pay for all of your dates, unless there's a huge disparity in the income range between you and the man. Even then you should be looking for ways to contribute to the relationship on a financial level. On the second meeting, assuming the man has initiated this and has asked you out on The Date, he will probably offer to pay and you should graciously accept. After the second date you should, at that point, offer to pay the entire tab or at least half of it as a way of saying thank you to him for paying for the previous meeting. To leave the best impression, you don't want it to appear that you are expecting him to foot the bill for the entire relationship. Most dating couples these days are sharing expenses pretty much fifty-fifty. This is not to say they are splitting every tab to the penny, but rather that if he pays for one dinner or night out, you would pay for the next.

That's it! Everything else, from how he dresses, whether or not he opens doors for you or knows which fork to use, are a matter of your personal tolerance. Just don't judge him on these things until you're absolutely certain he's in date mode.

Chapter 9
How Men Hunt Today

Now that you've read Chapter 5—What Men Want, you must realize that much of mating behavior is innate and instinctual, and has nothing to do with reason or rationale. This chapter is about another mating behavior that is innate and unconscious for men: hunting.

Over many eons, our foremothers made certain mating choices in order to ensure the survival of themselves and their offspring. One of these choices was to prefer men who were good providers rather than those who were not. Being a good provider has obvious reproductive value, and the way that men became good providers was by becoming good hunters. Hunting can be thought of as the single-minded pursuit of a valued object. The thing that makes an object valuable is scarcity. If the place were positively overflowing with game, then men wouldn't have to be very good at hunting in order to succeed, and hunting wouldn't have become as deep-seated a trait as it did.

Looking back at the statistics in Chapter 2, we learned that women were a valuable and scarce commodity in their twenties and even in their thirties. Young women can afford to be coy and demanding, and lead men on a good chase before they are actually acquired. There is an old saying, "Faint heart never won fair lady," which implies that only the most courageous men are likely to win the affections of the most desirable females. In other words, women get their pick of the best hunters, and the bad hunters don't get to reproduce their genes.

But all good things must come to an end. In our forties, women are about equal with men in terms of numbers, and by their fifties and sixties, women positively overrun the singles population. They are no longer a scarce commodity, therefore they are not as valuable *per se*, and consequently we can predict that men will not expend as much effort to acquire them as they would when they were younger.

In many cases, the hunter becomes the prey, as women who are desperate to attract men begin to hunt the depleted single male population like lionesses stalking a sick gazelle. At the other end of the spectrum, some women continue to act like they are still a scarce commodity and play the same types of mating games that they did when they were 25. Neither of these strategies is likely to succeed in attracting a long-term relationship.

Men need to hunt. If you are hunting them and deprive them of the opportunity to hunt you, then they will not define you as a valuable commodity, and will not value you when they catch you. On the other hand, there is no getting around the fact that there are many more single women than single men, and women are definitely not scarce at this age. So here is the challenge: notwith-standing that there are a lot of women out there for each man, how can you make the man of your choice understand that *there is only one of you* (ie, that you are a scarce commodity) and make him want to pursue *you*?

✌ LAW OF THE JUNGLE ✌
There may be a lot of women out there, but there is only one of YOU. Remember that.

In our focus groups and interviews with men, we found that, after age 40 and as high as age 70, men still need and expect to expend some effort to acquire a woman's affection. The hunting instinct goes deep, and is not extinguished as they age. However, while they are not averse to hunting women, they are no longer willing to put their lives or their egos on the line for them. With so many nice, attractive women out there, why would a man risk rejection or humiliation by pursuing a woman who does not wish to be pursued? Most men will only venture to pursue a woman who indicates at least some interest in him.

What Men Look For in a Date

Unlike women, who have many multidimensional criteria for accepting a mate, men generally have only a few criteria for women they are dating:

a. He must find her attractive

b. She must be attracted to him

c. They must have something in common

d. Her expectations regarding this date should match his own

The first criterion, that he must find her attractive, is the most important. Fortunately, we found that this is not difficult to achieve. Men tend to find many women attractive and interesting. If you follow the guidelines set out in Chapter 5 —What Men Want, you should do okay on this criterion.

A big finding in our interviews was that being *attracted* to him and letting him know it was just as important as making yourself *attractive* to him. At age 40 and over, men are just not willing to go to great lengths to chase after a woman unless they know ahead of time that they are going to have a good chance of catching her. Relationship economics is all about supply and demand. Many women fail to understand this. As we just discussed in the previous chapter, women are looking for that ideal date. They're looking for a man who doesn't commit any of the seven deadly dating sins. This means:

- ∞ Man picks her up at her home
- ∞ He's nicely and fashionably dressed
- ∞ They proceed to dinner, show, or other event, that the man has taken the initiative to come up with and make the arrangements for
- ∞ He is a complete gentleman and opens doors and pulls out chairs for her
- ∞ He displays impeccable table manners
- ∞ They have a meeting of the minds, chemistry is created, then
- ∞ He pays for both of them
- ∞ Man returns her to her house, possibly staying over, and
- ∞ Man calls the next day and/or sends flowers.

Needless to say, this hardly ever happens. He might stick his neck out and pay for dinner or pick her up at her door, but unless she is duly appreciative of his efforts, he will seek greener pastures. Some of the women we talked to refused to call their date afterwards to thank him for a nice time, or even refused to return his call. "I don't call men," we heard over and over again. Guess what? He doesn't need a brick wall to fall on him to see that it's going to be difficult to get anywhere with this type of woman. Why should he risk more rejection when it's so much easier just to ask someone else out?

Kim's Story

Kim is 48 years old and is out dating again for the first time after her twenty-year marriage ended a couple of years ago. Kim was introduced to Andrew. They went out on a Saturday. The meeting went quite well. Kim liked Andrew, and he suggested they get together again the following Wednesday. Andrew called Kim on Wednesday at 6:00 and suggested they get together at 8:00 that evening. Kim agreed, but after she hung up she thought about it and decided that she wasn't feeling totally comfortable with Andrew's suggestion. She would have had to drive about an hour to meet him and it was pouring rain. Kim called Andrew back and told him that she really didn't think that his suggestion was going to work. Andrew suggested that they get together the following night, Thursday, but he said it would have to be 8:00 or after because he was involved in a very big project at work with some tight deadlines. Kim, (who, by the way is fortunate enough not to have to work, so probably has more flexibility in her schedule) told Andrew that maybe he should call her in a week or so when he had more time.

Now Andrew asked Kim out two nights in a row. He was trying to make room for her in his busy schedule. Kim said no to both invitations. Do you think Andrew might have felt rejected? Do you think Andrew is going to bother calling Kim again in a week or so? Why would he risk the chance that she'd say no again? Kim was surprised when it was pointed out to her that she had just rejected Andrew twice, and if she was really as interested in him as she said she was, she was going to have to take the initiative to make the next move and call Andrew.

. . . .

✎ LAW OF THE JUNGLE ✎
What worked at age 20 no longer works at age 40 and over. It's time to grow up.

The third criterion is that the two of you must have something in common. Actually, this means that you must have something in common with *him*, and not the other way around. We know, we know... blame it on relationship economics. Often, an invitation to golf, ski, sporting events, movies, theatre, opera, and the like is a way of making these interests known to you, and your response is noted. They will also take note of whether you laugh at their jokes, and so on.

Our recommendation is that you do not lie about what interests you. If you are a dog hater and he suggests taking Fido out to the dog park one sunny afternoon, you don't have to do it. Remember, if the relationship works out, you will begin to hate Fido and resent having to live with him. What we are suggesting is that you remain open-minded to things that you haven't tried before. For instance, if he suggests golfing, you don't have to pretend to be an expert golfer. But if you like him, you may want to be flexible enough to say, "Gee, that sounds like fun. I'd like to try that." If your hobbies are traditionally feminine pursuits like knitting, sewing, quilting, book club, gardening, opera, or ballet, you may find that he is less than enthusiastic about volunteering to try them. We're afraid that you might have to continue to enjoy these activities on your own.

Finally, the fourth criterion is that your expectations for this particular date should be similar to his. Just because you are pretty, have a nice personality, and share a few interests does *not* mean that he will assume that the two of you will become a couple. If you make this assumption, you will be sadly disappointed. We have heard so many heartbreaking stories of dates where both laughed, talked into the wee hours of the night, had a real meeting of the minds—and then he never called her again. So do not fall into the trap of assuming that just because things went well that they will go further.

✎ LAW OF THE JUNGLE ✎

Most of the time, for men a date is just a date, not necessarily the beginning of a lifelong relationship. Men don't need a reason not to call you back. What they need is a reason to call you back.

CREATING RAPPORT

How do you let him know that you are attracted to him? You do it with certain visual and tactile cues. Men are not verbal creatures. It's women who try to extract information from what a man says, and very often are led astray by ambivalent phrases. Men do not try to analyze what women say. They respond more to eye movement (big eyes, lingering looks), facial expressions (smiles), and most tellingly, to small but communicative touches. And it doesn't take many of these clues to let him know that you're interested. Psychological research has shown that men tend to *overestimate* women's sexual interest while women tend to *underestimate* a man's willingness to commit.[35]

All of these things fall under the general category of "flirting." Interestingly, we encounter quite a few women who completely dismiss the concept of flirting. This is a mistake. If you want a man to understand your intentions, you must speak to him in a language he understands.

The first step in speaking this nonverbal language is to create rapport. Creating rapport is a good idea whenever you are dealing with either men or women, and works equally well with both sexes. People generally prefer to be with other people whom they view as being similar to themselves. One way that this similarity is judged is through body language and eye contact, which once again work at a more or less unconscious level. Here are a few simple exercises for creating rapport with another person at an unconscious level.

When you are creating rapport with another person, you are telling them at a subconscious level that "I am just like you," and increasing your chances of being accepted. At the most basic level, one way of creating rapport is by simple breathing. The next time you are together with another person, just try to match their

. . . .

35 Rebhahn, Peter, "Mixed signals – Research on gender differences in interpreting sexual signals," "Psychology Today," July 2000.

breathing pattern. Breathe in when they breathe in, and breathe out when they breathe out. That's all. Practice it.

Another simple exercise is to match another person's body posture. This works particularly well in business meetings, job interviews, or negotiations. Look at how they are sitting. What are their hands doing? Have they crossed their legs? Is the head tilted? Try to match this posture as closely as possible. When they move, you move too. Don't worry that they will get angry that you are mimicking them—they won't notice! It all happens below the level of awareness.

Finally, once you have the breathing and body posture down pat, listen to how they talk. Do they talk slowly and use a lot of kinesthetic words, "feeling" words? Do they speak fast and use a lot of visual imagery? What words are they using? Try and match them for speed and word content. Use the same words they are using.

These simple exercises can help you create rapport with anyone, anytime. They can help you meet people you want to attract as well as be on the same wavelength with people you already know. The next time you are at a party, look around and see if there's a person that you'd like to get to know, either man or woman. Use the techniques that you've practiced here and see how quickly you can create rapport with this person. Alternately, the next time you are on a date, try using these techniques with your date. People who are "in sync" have a better time together, and create more intimacy than people who aren't.

FLIRTING

Now that you've learned a bit about creating rapport, what about flirting? What is flirting? Webster's Dictionary says it's: a) to behave amorously without serious intent b) to show superficial or casual interest or liking.

Why do we *have* to flirt, especially over 40? Because it's imperative that you give men signals, in the way they understand them, that you're interested in them. We sometimes hear women say they don't know how to flirt and they don't think they should have to flirt. These women tend to feel that flirting is game-playing, it's not sincere, it's just not them. They also feel that a man should like them for who they are.

Don't forget: we're here to give you solid advice on how to increase your chances of finding a great man. Think of this in the same way you would if you were looking for a job. You might be an excellent employee, you might be the most qualified person for the job, but you're horrible at interviewing. If you're really serious about getting a job, you'll go out and figure out how to interview. Flirting is the same thing. It's another way of learning how to communicate that you're the best person for the job.

We often complain that men just don't communicate. But have we really learned their language? Have we learned how to communicate with them?

Just to recap, men over 40:

- want to avoid rejection
- are operating from a mentality of abundance and are in a position to do some cherry-picking
- are looking for a woman who is attracted to them
- are not willing to "chase" a woman who shows no interest in them.

So the question is how can you communicate to a man that you are attracted to him, you don't intend to reject him, and you are interested in him? How can you show him this? What are the "signs" men will get that a woman is interested?

While women tend to rely on verbal communication, men respond best to communication through *physical signals*. As we said before, these signals can come in the form of:

- ✍ eye movement (big eyes, lingering looks)
- ✍ facial expressions (smiles)
- ✍ leaning forward
- ✍ tilting of the head
- ✍ small but communicative touches are the most telling (a touch on the back of the hand or arm, a touch on the knee, a playful kick).

Can you practice flirting? Yes! And if you feel like you just don't know how to flirt, or you're not comfortable flirting, you *need* to practice. Remember, flirting is not serious. It should be fun, light, and playful. Flirting is about making the person you're flirting with feel good about themselves. It's about letting someone else know that you recognize their value as a person, as a fellow human being. It's about letting the other person know that you respect their knowledge or expertise in a specific area.

The following are exercises you can do to practice flirting.

Start by making a list of ten non-threatening people you can flirt with. These might be people like a parking lot attendant, a waiter (gay men are usually particularly easy and wonderful to practice flirting with), a concierge in an office building, a store clerk, etc.

Ten non-threatening people who are easy to flirt with:

1. _____

2. _____

3. _____

4. _____

5. _____

6. _____

7. _____

8. _____

9. _____

10. _____

Exercise 1.

Practice making three strangers a day smile, just by making eye contact and smiling at them. Do this every day for at least a week, or until you feel quite comfortable smiling at strangers and getting a smile in response.

Exercise 2.

Practice saying something nice to someone new every day. This could be a compliment, or it could be a slightly more personal, informal question. Example: instead of saying the perfunctory "Hi, how are you?" you could say "Good morning, John. How's your day going today?" Pay particular attention to your tone of voice. Make it light, positive, upbeat. Be sure you're smiling, and be certain to make eye contact.

Exercise 3.

Practice asking for help from someone you might not usually ask for help. People love helping others because it makes them feel competent and needed. For example, practice with a waiter asking for his opinion. In a playful way, you might say "You know, I just can't decide for the life of me if I should have the chicken supreme or the pasta special. I'm sure you're a culinary expert. What would you recommend?"

Exercise 4.

Choose three of the ten people above. Think about how you can make your next conversation with that person flirtatious. Then just do it!

THE KEY TO FLIRTING SUCCESS

There are four things to remember when flirting:

1. Feel comfortable with yourself.

2. Genuinely appreciate, value, and/or respect the other person.

3. Understand that flirting is not proposing marriage.

4. Have fun!

Chapter 10

The Big Question

In a recent episode of a reality TV show, men and women were deposited on some tropical resort island and were supposed to partner up with each other on contrived "dates" with total strangers, then do follow-up date post-mortems with a secret camera. Bachelor #1, a tanned, good-looking young man, was speaking into the camera about his date with Bachelorette #1, who was very pretty by conventional standards, but about average for the contestants on this show. He talked about her sense of humor, her kindness, her intelligence, and many other sterling qualities which she possessed. He then talked about Bachelorette #2, a stunning blonde whom he found very attractive sexually, but did not really "click" with on any other level. The corresponding interview with Bachelorette #1 indicated that she also found her time with him to be enjoyable and rewarding. In fact, they had had a real "meeting of the minds" and she was beginning to fall in love with him. In the next segment of the show, Bachelor #1 was given a choice between the two women. The one he chose would continue as a contestant in the show, and he would have an opportunity to date her again, and the one not chosen would go home. The two women stood there side by side while he made up his mind. Bachelorette #1 stood confident and sure of her man, with a twinkle in her eye, remembering all that had passed between them the night before. Bachelorette #2 sucked in her stomach and thrust forward her ample bosom. "Well," said Bachelor #1, "It was a tough decision, but my choice is… Bachelorette #2." Bachelorette #1 was visibly stunned! She began to cry, and in the post-mortem interview sobbed that she was completely baffled by his choice. They had had such intimacy together, had talked about everything, and had such fun. She had really thought this relationship could go somewhere, and so on.

To us, this episode represents a microcosm of the innate differences between men and women when it comes to sexual attraction and relationships. Bachelorette #1 felt that she was falling in love with Bachelor #1. But it wasn't because he was buff and tanned and good-looking (although that certainly didn't hurt). It was because they had talked, and shared, and laughed together that she found him so compelling. On his part, Bachelor #1 acknowledged all of these things, but in the end he preferred the woman whom he found more physically attractive.

In our interviews with women, we asked how they knew when they wanted to have sex with a man. The answer was invariably that there had to be "chemistry" between them. Women were not interested in having sex unless there was chemistry, and were very likely to end budding relationships which did not look as if any chemistry could be created for them, even if the men wanted to continue with it. Obviously, chemistry is very important. What does it mean?

Chemistry has a number of components for women. It can mean any or all of the following. It should be noted that, if any of the necessary criteria are absent, women will generally not wish to progress to a sexual relationship:

a. Liking and respect for the man; self-confidence and presentation; kindness, generosity, protectiveness, chivalry and other positive traits; personal acceptability in terms of status, income, personality, and so on.

b. The possibility that the relationship will continue; that some potential exists to make it permanent; that this man could be a suitable life partner for them and they can visualize what their future together would look like.

c. That the man is willing to commit to a monogamous relationship; that his affections are not otherwise engaged by an ex-wife or current girlfriend.

d. That there is at least some physical attraction on both sides, or rather, that there are no physical turn-offs.

Whew! No wonder men are so confused about what women want. The least important criterion on this list is physical attractiveness. It's not that women don't care about beauty; it's just that it's not enough to convince them to have sex. If you read Chapter 5—What Men Want, you will remember that women assess attractiveness in a different way than men, so it will come as no surprise that their standards for what makes a suitable sexual partner are also different.

Besides personal acceptability in terms of appearance and character, women need to feel that there is at least some chance that the relationship will move forward. If they can project themselves into the future and visualize a positive relationship with this man, then they will consider him as a sexual partner. When they cannot see a future with this man, women will tend to stop dating him, even if it means they will be alone. The women we interviewed were adamant on this point. They described experiences where they knew there was no future but had sex anyway as empty and unfulfilling. Women will not stay long in relationships which, to them, are pointless. And sex for the sake of sex is ultimately pointless to most women.

BEFORE WE GO ANY FURTHER, I NEED TO
KNOW IF YOU LOVE ME.

The other important ingredient in the chemistry formula is
investment. Women are looking for *investment* from their potential
sexual partners. By investment, we mean that the man is willing
to expend emotional and material resources for their benefit. For
instance, an emotional investment might consist of cuddling,
talking, kindness, acts of service, love talk, foreplay, and generally taking an interest in things which make her happy. Material
investment might be gift-giving, generosity, paying for dinner,
and having a good job and adequate income. To women, these
things imply that the man is interested in them as potential mates
and will not be skipping town after getting them into bed. There
must be both the ability to invest emotionally and materially, as
well as the willingness. A besotted suitor who is dirt poor is of little
interest, as is a wealthy man who is cold and ungenerous. In the

former, the man has the willingness but not the means, and in the latter there is the means but not the willingness.

In the reality show example, Bachelorette #1 was confused about the man's choice because she had interpreted his actions of the night before as a willingness to invest in her. For all we know he might have been, until the prettier alternative came along and he realized he had a shot at Bachelorette #2.

Men, on the other hand, do not have multiple criteria for choosing sex partners. For men, it boils down to sexual attractiveness and willingness on the part of the woman. For many men, sex is just sex, and there is nothing wrong with that.

While men seek out lovers who are sexually attractive, and only after sex decide if they're going to invest further in them, women seek out men who appear to be acceptable *and* who show a willingness to invest in them, and only then do they decide if they're going to have sex with them.[36] Men and women are basically approaching sex from opposite ends of the spectrum.

If men were allowed to behave according to their preference, sex would be a starting point, whereas for women, it would be an end point. Where they end up is a function of the negotiation that takes place between them. Women may offer sex if they see some evidence of investment. And men may offer investment if they see a chance of sex. Men will only invest as much as they need to up front in order to get sex.[37] In the past, this could well have been marriage. But since the invention of oral contraceptives,

. . . .

36   Townsend, John, *What Women Want – What Men Want: Why The Sexes Still See Love & Commitment So Differently*, Oxford University Press, 1998, pg. 119.

37   Ibid pg 23

the investment required has gone down dramatically. The consequences of compliance are very much less for women now.

The formula for chemistry can thus be summarized as:

Women

$$\frac{\text{Man's personal acceptability} + \text{potential for the future} + \text{evidence of emotional investment} + \text{capability for material investment}}{\text{chemistry for sex}}$$

Men

$$\frac{\text{Woman's sexual attractiveness and willingness}}{\text{chemistry for sex}}$$

It is these differences which make women crazy. They tend to think that men are simply underdeveloped, less evolved versions of themselves. They try to apply the same logic to men's behavior as they do to their own, and come to the conclusion that men must be childish, immoral louts. Television sitcoms tend to reinforce this image of men for women. It becomes the woman's role to guide the man to appropriate behavior and ways of thinking. Occasionally we hear women say that they want a man "who has done some work on himself." Ask any man what that means and he'll tell you that the guy is probably going to the gym more often to work out. It does *not* mean that he sees a psychotherapist regularly to help him work through his feelings. Men will generally not do that kind of work until they find themselves in the "cosmic frying pan:" facing a big loss of some kind in terms of family, money, job, home, or something like that.

Again, we have said this before but it bears repeating: men are just different. The more research that is done into male-female differences, the more clear it becomes that many of these differences are beyond cultural. They are innate, biological differences resulting from the way men and women evolved over millions of years.

✑ LAW OF THE JUNGLE ✑

Men and women are innately different. You cannot apply the same logic to a man's behavior as you can to your own.

Needless to say, we are telling you here and now that the psychology of men is very different to that of women, and nowhere is it more different than when it comes to sex. When women interpret men's actions by their own logic, they end up misinterpreting behavior, making bad decisions, and getting really hurt in some cases.

We are telling you this because to be forewarned is to be forearmed. Understanding how men approach sex in relationships enables you to make better choices when it comes to sexual relations while dating. Sex is one thing that can make you feel great or horrible about yourself and affect your self-confidence, so it's important to understand how men and women think about it before you decide if you're going to have sex or not.

Annette's Story

Annette had been out with Ron four or five times and really liked him. Ron had been calling her every day since they first met [evidence of emotional investment]. According to Annette, Ron was very good looking, there was plenty of physical attraction, and he was the nicest, sweetest, most sincere man she had met [evidence of personal acceptability]. He was a "really, really decent guy." He was an absolutely lovely man, and he was serious about wanting to find the right woman and get married [further evidence of emotional investment and willingness to commit to a monogamous relationship]. Annette had been to Ron's home and was quite impressed. He lived in a very nice townhouse, beautifully decorated, and he drove a very good, expensive car [evidence of capability for material investment].

It was the holiday season and Annette had accepted an invitation to Ron's house for New Year's Eve. After thinking about this, Annette called Ron back to say she'd changed her mind. She knew that she would be drinking, and she would end up spending the night at Ron's house. She also knew that the physical attraction was mutual, and that if she ended up staying the night they'd have sex. Annette said she just couldn't do that because she didn't see any future in the relationship. As much as she liked him, was physically attracted to him and thought he was really wonderful, she just felt they were too different and she couldn't allow herself to go down the road of having sex with him. There was just one part of the equation that was missing for her: the potential for the future.

. . . .

Annette made a very wise decision for her own protection. Not all of us are always that wise. Sometimes we fall into traps. Here are some common traps that women fall into. These are all traps because one or more of the ingredients required for good sexual chemistry are missing, making them less than favorable experiences.

THE TRAP OF THE PERFECT DATE

Picture this scenario. You are on a first or second date with a man you really like and seem to have a lot in common with. You are having a wonderful time, and there is no end in sight to this date. You end up back at his place (or your place) and talk for hours, you laugh and listen to music, and you feel as though this man could really be The One. You make love, and in the morning he swears that he will call you. You have visions of repeating the whole perfect experience with him, but for some reason, he doesn't call you the next day. No emails, no card, no flowers arriving at your door. You wonder if he's gotten into an accident on the way home, but later learn that was not the case. He simply doesn't call and you never hear from him again.

Many, many women we have interviewed have fallen into this trap. They imagine that they must have done something wrong and analyze the evening with their girlfriends trying to figure out what they did to chase him away. Either that or they blame themselves for being stupid and not realizing he was a jerk. Then they feel victimized, and instead of looking back at the evening as romantic and wonderful, it becomes an embarrassing, confusing experience.

All of the ingredients of sexual chemistry were there, or appeared to be there: personal acceptability, a possible future together, and investment. Unfortunately, you mistook the investment he made to get you into bed as investment into a *relationship*, and you played your best card right away. There is no possibility of a future together and no further investment, which makes this experience bad all around.

Now, you could see it as the man being a jerk and manipulating you into having sex. Or, to look at it from a man's point of view, you could say that the evening was complete and perfect in itself. It was romantic and fun, and ended with sex. What more could a guy wish for? There will be lots of fond memories there. There is nothing wrong with you, and you didn't do anything wrong. He may have intended to call you again, but afterwards he decided that he did not want to make any further investment, so he didn't. Period.

The Trap of One-Night Stands and Casual Sex

In general, we are against the practice of one-night stands and casual sex. Oh, it's not what you think. We are not judging the practice as immoral nor do we feel that a woman who does it is a slut. No, no. The reason we are against one-night stands is because *you probably won't enjoy it and will probably not look back on it with enjoyment.*

Studies on American women have found that, not only do women prefer sex when they are in committed, loving relationships, they are actually more likely to orgasm in these types of relationships rather than in casual encounters.[38] The reason is due to the basic psychology of sex. The investment and possible future components are missing; therefore the full chemistry of the moment is not present, which means a lower-level sexual experience.

Unfortunately, casual sex is the type of thing one sometimes has to do in order to discover that one doesn't like it, sort of like eating oysters. It falls into the category of things that seemed like a good idea at the time, but afterwards you regret it.

THE TRAP OF FRIENDS WITH BENEFITS

Friends with benefits is a modern concept that appears to be brilliant at first glance. Two people who know each other, are maybe friends or past lovers, come together to gratify their physical needs in mutual, honest, and equal consent. How does it get any better than that? You are not having sex with a stranger, so the guesswork and any potential danger is eliminated. It's all comfortable and good. Nothing to do but sit back and enjoy it, right?

Once again, though, we have two missing ingredients in the chemistry formula: investment and a possible future together. Your partner may be willing to invest something in you for as long as it takes to have sex, and then he's gone. Back to being just good friends. There is no future, no long-term prospect, no commitment, and no investment. In short, there is no point to it. Women who have had friends with benefits often find that these types of relationships are very difficult to manage, because in the absence

. . . .
38   Ibid pg. 15

of investment, they try to *create* investment. They can't help themselves: investment is what makes the experience satisfying rather than pointless. They may even (horrors) convince themselves that they are in love with their partner and begin to make demands which were not part of the original bargain. Then they are sadly disappointed when he does not want to deal with that, and that's the end of the friend with benefits.

The Trap of Dating Stringers

This is the worst trap of all. It would be impossible to overestimate the danger posed by Stringers to your self-confidence and sanity. Stringers are men who are not interested in a committed monogamous relationship with any woman, but who lead you to believe that they could be if the right woman came along. They might tell you straight out that they are confirmed bachelors and want to date other people. Or, at the other end of the spectrum, they may say that they are looking for a mate, but she has been so hard to find. They may tell you about other previous relationships where they thought they had found love but it just wasn't the right person. Or, that they want to carry the relationship forward, but they are still married and awaiting a divorce, or can't get a divorce because of the children, or something like that.

The reason this is a trap is that so many women believe that THEY will succeed where so many others have failed. They reason that, if you can have sex with them and make them "yours," you are more likely to be able to keep them and fix their emotional wounds. The result is that you could end up having sex and wasting your time with someone who is not willing or able to invest in you, or who spreads their investment so thin that you will never be able to get enough to meet your needs. You are simply strung along for as long as you care to believe in him, trying hard to make the relationship work so that you can be The One for him. If the idea of constantly having to fight off competitors or share your man with other women doesn't appeal to you, learn to recognize Stringers and avoid them like the plague.

Unlike friends with benefits or casual sex partners, Stringers do offer a type of investment in you as well as a future together. They may take you out, talk, give gifts and so on. But their investment is always partial, because they spread it around to other women as well as you, and are not willing to commit. And the future is always on their terms and not yours. Therefore, the chemistry required for sex is always incomplete; you end up starving on crumbs.

How do you know if you're dating a Stringer? Before you have sex with him, look for any of these signs:

- He is married.
- He has been separated for a while but not divorced, and doesn't seem to be able to agree with the ex so that a divorce can be completed.
- He has never been married, or married at some early point, but since then he has had a series of monogamous relationships which have ended.
- He is dating two or more women right now. When he's with you though, he acts as if you're the best.
- He tells you straight out that he does not want to be monogamous, that he wants to date different people.
- He says that none of his previous girlfriends were right; they were all missing something.
- He says he will understand if you cannot deal with his dating other women, and advises you to do what you have to do, even if it means moving on.

All in all, a bad formula for sexual chemistry.

Christina's Story

Christina met Alan through mutual friends. Alan was married and Christina had even met his wife. There were a group of friends who hung out together because they were on the same softball team. Alan was one of the group. Christina thought Alan was funny and a good guy, but didn't think much about him because he was married. Over the course of several months of playing softball together Alan started flirting with Christina and gradually started to share his sad story about his marriage. There really wasn't anything left of the marriage and there hadn't been for many years. Alan and his wife had separate bedrooms and lived in separate sides of the house. The situation was quite complicated because they owned a very large business together, and the marriage was really a business partnership. Christina actually started feeling sorry for Alan, and a close friendship was forming. They had lots in common and really connected. Alan eventually asked Christina if she'd like to have dinner with him on a non-softball night. Christina said yes, because after all, this wasn't really a date, they were just friends, and she wanted to help Alan resolve his situation. Christina ended up having sex with Alan that very first night after their dinner. There was huge chemistry, they really connected mentally, emotionally, and physically and Christina could see how much Alan wanted to be free of his marriage.

Christina had a "relationship" with Alan, but actually she thought of him as a project; she wanted to fix him. Over the course of time she and Alan got closer and closer. She found out that Alan had over twenty-five affairs during the course of his marriage, and he had a son with one of the women with whom he had had an affair. This son was the apple of Alan's eye. Alan was good to his son and the mother of his son. He took very good care of them financially. Christina saw that there were definitely challenges in her relationship with Alan, they couldn't see each other openly and freely, but they were making so much progress. Alan was really different with her. She was the first woman he had ever shared these secrets with. She was the only woman who had ever met his son. In fact, the three of them spent lots of time together. They even had a Christmas together a day or so after Christmas. Christina was smitten with Alan and his son and could see a wonderful family life in the future. Christina was really helping Alan get his life together. She helped him look for a piece of property, which he ended up buying. Alan was going to build a new home on the property so he could finally move out of the house with his wife, get a divorce, have a home to which he could freely bring his son, and move forward with his life. Christina spent hours with Alan looking at magazine pictures of homes they liked and creating a vision of a dream home. She even found an architect and she and Alan met with the architect together. There was lots of promise. Alan was really different with Christina. She was really helping him. She was making a difference in his life.

Fourteen months into the relationship Alan decided that it was all too much. He told Christina that his life was too complicated. He had two women he needed to worry about, his wife and the mother of his son. He just couldn't see how he could really take on a third woman in his life. Alan was a first-class Stringer. All of the signs were there. Like so many women, however, Christina deluded herself into believing that she could change him. With her, Alan was really different. Christina had created in her mind the formula with Alan. He was personally acceptable, there was potential for the future, there was evidence of emotional investment, and there was the capability for material investment, so there was chemistry for sex. Unfortunately, the only place the formula existed was in Christina's mind. Christina now looks back on this situation with twenty-twenty hindsight and says "What was I thinking?"

. . . .

⊱ LAW OF THE JUNGLE ⊰

If he looks like a Stringer, walks like a Stringer, talks like a Stringer, acts like a Stringer, he's a Stringer. Do NOT delude yourself! Millions have gone before you.

Okay, so you're dating a wonderful man, there is real chemistry there, and you decide to go for it. Great! Yikes! "Where's my 21-year-old body?" "I haven't had sex with a man other than my ex-husband in over twenty years!" "What do I do now?" "Oh my gosh, do I really have to get naked for this?" "Maybe we can turn the lights off." "What if he can't perform?"

If you've heard yourself thinking or saying any of these things, you're not alone. Women we have interviewed about their sexual practices have told us that there are two issues which cause anxiety: sexual performance and discussion of sexual matters.

Sexual Performance

Take heart! According to Dr. Trina Read, sexologist,[39] having sex is like riding a bicycle. Your knowledge of how to have sex does not go away, even if you haven't had sex in a long time. We all come to the table with a bag of sex tricks. Don't worry about your sexual performance or how you might compare to other lovers he's had. Men will take an enthusiastic bed partner over a hot babe who just lies there any day. So, as Dr. Read says, you "gotta shake what your momma gave ya."

For sex to be successful a man must have an orgasm – that's what we have all been conditioned to think. Unfortunately, this is not as easy for men at age 50 as it was at age 20. Cardiovascular disease, diabetes, hypertension, smoking, alcohol usage, hypercholesterolaemia and NSAIDs all contribute to erectile dysfunction, and incidence of ED increases with age: from twelve

. . . .

39   Interview with Dr. Trina Read, Sexologist.

cases per thousand for men aged 40 to 49, to 46 cases per thousand for men aged 60 to 69.[40] So for your sake and his, it is important to increasingly try and shift attention away from his orgasm to just having fun and sharing intimacy.

For women especially, it's really about self-confidence and knowing what your own comfort level is. To thine own self be true. Dr. Read suggests that if you're concerned about your no-longer-20-year-old-body, you buy a piece of lingerie that you feel comfortable in and use candles instead of total darkness. There are also lots of books, classes, and workshops on sex. Many of these are extremely tastefully done, and very helpful.[41]

DISCUSSION OF SEXUAL MATTERS

We don't care how old you are, if you're going to have sex with someone, you MUST consider the issue of sexually transmitted diseases and HIV. According to the National Institute on Aging, 19 percent of people in the U.S. who are HIV positive are over 50 years of age, as are 10 to15 percent of all AIDS patients. It's NOT just a disease of young people. Just because you were in a monogamous relationship for twenty years does NOT make you immune to sexually transmitted diseases today.

Monica's Story

Monica is a petite, attractive, and chic woman in her forties. She was married for many years but is now divorced. Then she was in a monogamous relationship with a man, but recently that ended. Now she is dating again. She went out on a date with a man she had known in the past as a friend, but with whom she was never sexually involved. Now he lives in another country, but travels often to

. . . .

40   Jahannes, CD, Araujo, AB, Feldman, HA, Denby, CA, Kleinman, KP, and McKinlay, JB, "Incidence of erectile dysfunction in men 40 to 69 years old: longitudinal results from the Massachusetts male aging study," in *Journal of Urology*, 2000; 163(2):460-3

41   See Dr. Read's website for more ideas and advice at www.trina-read.com.

her city. They were not strangers to each other, and he hinted on their first date that he would like to become intimate with her. She resisted. On the second date, he made himself very clear that he wanted to have sex, and she consented on the proviso that he use a condom. Unfortunately, a condom was not to be found at that time of the night either for love or money, so despite her better judgement, Monica had sex with him anyway.

. . . .

Now, whether or not it was all right in the end, Monica was really taking a stupid and unnecessary chance with her health. At the end of the day, she did not know this man from a brick in the wall, nor his sexual history. She worried about the consequences of unprotected sex well after the moment had passed.

Monica is not unique in allowing herself to be persuaded into having unprotected sex. In an ideal world, men and women would discuss these things beforehand and show each other a clean bill of health. However, almost none of the women we interviewed ever did this. Somehow, talking about sex is harder than having sex and worrying about it afterwards. Sometimes you're lucky, but sometimes you're not.

We know that even though you know you should talk with your partner about sex beforehand, you probably won't. So we are not going to preach to you about this (at least, no more than we've already done). We are simply going to INSIST that you do not have unprotected sex until such a discussion and/or examination takes place. Even if that means that you carry condoms around in your purse.

✑ LAW OF THE JUNGLE ✑

You've got to protect yourself. You shouldn't be dying to have sex.

NOT ONLY DO WE KNOW WITHIN THE
FIRST FEW SECONDS WHETHER HE HAS A
CHANCE WITH US OR NOT, WE ALSO
KNOW EXACTLY HOW MANY DATES IT
WILL TAKE FOR SAID CHANCE TO OCCUR.

Chapter 11

How Do You Know If You've Found Mr. Right?

BLINK, THINK, OR BOTH?

How do you really know if you've found Mr. Right? Do you just *know*? Is it completely intuitive, based on a gut feel, or is it something you have to seriously think about and analyze? Is there a list of pros and cons you need to carefully weigh? Do you feel that you've made mistakes in other relationships? You *thought* you had found Mr. Right, but clearly you were wrong because that relationship didn't last. Well, we think it's a combination of both blink and think. The question is when are we blinking, or going with the initial reaction, and when are we thinking, weighing, and analyzing the information?

We've said it before, but we can't tell you how many men and women we hear say that they just know in the first thirty to sixty seconds of meeting someone if there's any chemistry. Lots of people are making decisions that affect the rest of their lives based on thirty to sixty seconds worth of "information." The question is just how useful are these instant reactions?

Many of us have had one of those hot and heavy romances where there was instant chemistry and lots of mad passion. But did they always last? For almost everyone reading this book, the answer to that question would be no, or we assume you wouldn't be here now. So why do we continue to rely on our gut reactions to make our decisions about dating a man if our past experience hasn't served us too well?

Malcolm Gladwell, in his recent book *Blink*, talks about "the power of thinking without thinking." Gladwell discusses the process of "thin-slicing," which is "the ability of our unconscious mind to find patterns in situations and behavior based on very narrow slices of experience."[42] He gives interesting examples of when thin-slicing has worked and when it hasn't. We all thin-slice, we can't help it. It's part of what we do as human beings. We use it to protect ourselves. A thin slice can tell us an awful lot about a situation.

Gladwell presents some findings from a study done on speed-dating in New York. He talks about speed-dating being the distillation of dating to a simple snap judgment. Everyone who is speed-dating is trying to answer a very simple question: Do I want to see this person again? Most of our clients say they don't like the idea of speed-dating at all. It's ridiculous to think you can tell

. . . .

42   Gladwell, Malcolm, *Blink*, Little, Brown and Company, New York, 2005 pg. 23.

much about someone in just three minutes. And yet, many of those same people who don't like the idea of speed-dating are doing their own version of it every time they go out to meet a new man. They even say they know in the first couple of minutes if there's anything there.

Interestingly, in the speed-dating study, the researchers found that people would say they were looking for certain characteristics and attributes in a potential partner, for example a sense of humor, sincerity, or intelligence, but it was just as likely that the people they were attracted to and chose in their speed-experience didn't have a great sense of humor, and weren't particularly sincere or smart at all. So people say they want one thing, but are frequently attracted to something else. The explanation for this, according to Gladwell, is that the description a person starts with is their conscious ideal: what they think they want when they sit down and think about it. But what they cannot be certain about are the criteria they use to form their preferences in that first instant of meeting someone face-to-face. That information is locked behind the door of the subconscious mind.

Our explanations of what we're looking for in a man often do not match with whom we are attracted in the moment. As Gladwell says "we have, as human beings, a storytelling problem. We're a bit too quick to come up with explanations for things we don't really have an explanation for."[43] He goes on to say that we have to accept that there are times when we can know more about someone or something based on first impressions, in the blink of an eye, than we can after months of study. "But we also have to acknowledge and understand those circumstances when rapid cognition leads us astray."[44]

This is our concern. We don't deny that everyone is looking for "chemistry." However, it seems that too many women are severely

....

43   Ibid. pg. 69

44   Ibid. pg. 76

hurting their chances of finding a truly wonderful man, because they're not aware of when "thin-slicing" is leading them astray. There has to be attraction, but that attraction isn't always instantaneous. It can grow over time as you get to know a man. Think how much you could increase your odds of being in a great relationship with a man if you would just give more men a chance.

Let's say you meet an incredible man. He's extremely good-looking and you both definitely feel that sexual attraction. Wonderful. The only problem is that it doesn't matter if this man is drop-dead gorgeous. It's a scientific fact that the body creates a whole concoction of "love drugs" throughout the initial phases of a relationship. These chemicals will be produced in the body for twelve to twenty-four months. These "drugs" are responsible for that euphoric "in love" feeling which puts us in that romance phase of our relationships. When these "love drugs" wear off, when the body stops producing them; it doesn't matter if your man is Sean Connery, Harrison Ford, Tom Cruise, or Brad Pitt. That incredible attractiveness just won't be enough anymore. The thrill is gone. This is when you realize that maybe your blink decision wasn't based on quite enough information to sustain a long-term relationship.

This is why we recommend a combination of "think" and "blink" when it comes to dating and relationships. If we, as women, could just think a little bit more in those first thirty to sixty seconds, and not rely totally on our "blink" instincts, we'd be more successful in our quest to find a man. Remember, as we mentioned earlier, when emotions are high, as they definitely are when you first meet a man, intelligence is low. Don't allow yourself to make a potential life-altering decision by "thin-slicing" at this point. You could be terribly wrong. You could cross the most wonderful man off your list, one you could fall madly in love with if you gave it a chance.

LAW OF THE JUNGLE

When you first meet a man, don't "blink," think. Don't allow yourself to completely judge a book by its cover. Give yourself the chance to at least read the first few chapters.

In the long run, after you've had an opportunity to get to know someone for who they truly are, your instincts, your heart, will definitely tell you what is right. Even Gladwell talks about the difference between a blink moment and the miracle of a *pure* blink moment. The *pure* blink moments are those when our prejudices and our preconceived notions are set aside and "we take charge of the first two seconds" of our experiences.[45] This is when we see people for who they truly are.

As we discussed in Chapter 7, most of dating today, with the use of speed-dating, online dating, singles events, and dating services, creates a "manufactured" environment. Because dating is backwards, our processes are backwards. We used to think (we got to know a guy through friends, or classes at school), then blink (we felt that gut level feeling of attraction, because we got to know him). Now we blink (decide in the first thirty to sixty seconds of a blind date if there's any attraction or chemistry) then we think. The thinking we do now is an afterthought. We're really coming up with a justification, or an intellectual alibi for why we are, or are not, attracted to this man.

Angela's Story

Angela is a divorced senior-level executive, with no kids, who has lots of responsibility and pressure in her job. She works long hours and has a big six-figure income. She owns her own home and drives a luxury car. She has a very specific list of things she's looking for in a man. He has to be well educated, as successful as

45 Ibid. pg. 254

she is, or more so; a "corporate-type" who is equally committed to his job, someone she can talk business with and can understand and appreciate her life and her work pressures. Like her, she wants someone who enjoys the finer things in life and is not cheap. It would also be great if he were a golfer.

Angela met Robert. Robert meets *none* of Angela's criteria, except that he plays golf. Robert has never worked a day in the corporate, or for that matter, the business world. Robert makes under six figures, and always has. Robert doesn't drive a luxury car. He works shifts, he's winding down his work life, and only works about eighty days a year. He'll be eligible for early retirement in his late fifties in a year or so. Angela called to "report in" on her way home after she had met Robert for the first time. She couldn't control herself. She was positively giddy. She couldn't get over the chemistry and attraction. "Oh my god, he's so gorgeous! It was all I could do to control myself and not ask him to come back to my place." They had such a good time. They talked, they laughed, they had fun. It was so easy. But she was confused because she wasn't supposed to be attracted to this kind of man. He didn't meet her criteria. Then the intellectual alibis began. Even though he's not the corporate type, he's so intelligent. You'd never know he does what he does for a living. But you really have to be very smart to be up on everything he knows for his job. Even though he doesn't make a lot of money, he's saved and has a decent lifestyle. He's got a lot of time on his hands, so he could take care of things around the house. I could probably live with someone taking care of me so I never had to worry about plumbing, or changing light bulbs again.

. . . .

This just happened two weeks before this was written, so it's way too early to know if Angela and Robert will ever actually make it. It was, however, very interesting to witness the process. First there was the instant blink reaction of Angela that Robert was hot, hot, hot! There was probably a quick jolt of love drugs going on to add to the scenario. The information locked behind the closed door of Angela's subconscious mind said "YES, YES, YES!" Whatever unconscious patterns are there in Angela's brain apparently matched pretty darn well with whatever Robert presented. Then after the "date," the conscious brain kicked in, it started thinking, and said, "But wait, he doesn't match *'the list'*, my rapid cognition might be leading me astray." This was followed very quickly by an extensive list of rationalizations and justifications for the attraction.

That's one interesting thing about how people make decisions. The more important the decision, the less likely one is to make it based on logic. The unconscious mind takes a belief (Angela only likes men who are successful, ambitious, well educated), and builds a reality around it (Angela only dates these types of men). When a dissonant event happens (Angela really likes Robert, who does not exactly fit the type), the unconscious mind *does not* change its reality if it can avoid doing so. Instead, it forms an intellectual alibi in order to fit the dissonant component into the existing belief system (Robert is successful, ambitious and well educated – in his own way).

In this case, Angela has jumped right in and was instantly smitten. She couldn't wait to see Robert again. Based on our theories of compatibility (which we'll get to shortly), it's highly unlikely that there's enough there to build a lasting relationship on. It could have just as easily happened in the reverse, that there wasn't any instant chemistry, but lots of things to build on in terms of values and compatibility. In this case, Angela would have, and in fact has in the past, decided right away that she didn't want to see the person again. This is a perfect example of where we feel it would be incredibly helpful to think first, *then* blink. Why do we almost literally jump at some situations that make little or no sense, and drop another opportunity that has lots of potential like a hot potato?

When we were in our twenties and hanging out in a group, there may have been some guy who liked us, but we thought he was a bit nerdy, or not as cute as some other guy. Over time we got to know him because we were all hanging out together. Eventually, we started to like him; maybe he was kind of cute after all. Then we started dating and a relationship ensued. Have you ever had one of those experiences? Probably a lot of us have. Today, although we desperately need to give ourselves these opportunities because meeting men is so much more difficult, we don't. We blink, and go with that knee-jerk reaction and cross the man with lots of potential off the list. Don't get us wrong. We're not proposing for a second that you settle for something that isn't great. We're not suggesting that you should just forget about wanting to have that zing of the sexual attraction. We think you should definitely have it. But we also know that the zing can grow as you get to know someone. We also know that the zing can fizzle just about as fast as it came.

There's much more to a relationship than just that initial zing and chemistry. Many of us have been in relationships where there was lots of chemistry but not enough compatibility. Generally speaking, the more we have in common when it comes to values, socio-economic demographics, and shared interests and activities, the better it is for the long-term happiness and health of the relationship. There are areas, however, where opposites very often attract.

EXERCISE

List below the names of each partner in ten couples. These would be couples that you personally are acquainted with.

1. _____   _____

2. _____   _____

3. _____   _____

4. _____   _____

5. _____   _____

6. _____   _____

7. _____   _____

8. _____   _____

9. _____   _____

10. _____   _____

Now, go back for each person in the couple and put an 'E' beside their name if they are an extrovert, and an 'I' beside their name if they are an introvert. We think you'll probably find that at least 70 percent of the time one partner is definitely more extroverted than the other. This is one area in which opposites tend to attract.

It's fascinating that in interviews with hundreds of singles, 80 percent or more of introverts say they want an extrovert. They're looking for someone who can draw them out a bit. An extrovert usually doesn't say they're looking for an introvert, but if they're questioned on it they would probably agree that they could be with someone less extroverted than themselves. We're usually subconsciously looking for balance in our lives. Just as the extrovert might help bring the introvert to life, the introvert may enable the extrovert to shine while providing a solid support.

There are lots of ways in which we may be drawn to someone who is the opposite of what we are. Again, this is usually something that we're not even conscious of. The challenge with this is that those very things that are the opposite characteristics to what we have, that we're attracted to, are the very things that will cause friction and tension in the relationship in the long haul. In other words, the cute little quirky things that we loved about someone initially are probably the things that will drive us crazy about them after the love drugs wear off. The more we're aware of who we are and what characteristics and values are the strongest and most important to us, and the more we understand about a potential partner prior to making a long-term commitment, the better off we'll be.

You may find that one partner is more detail-oriented than the other, one might be more spontaneous than the other, or one might be more active than the other. We're not looking for clones of ourselves, but the more we have in common, the more shared values we have, the more our partner fits our subconscious patterns of what a partner is supposed to be, the easier the relationship will be.

We've developed a proprietary tool which we call the Masterful Matchmaker Assessment. This assessment measures personality traits, values, and behaviors in twelve different areas to help you understand the traits that most strongly influence your compatibility with a partner and the characteristics and values in a mate that will provide you with sustainable happiness. It's been interesting to see how effective this tool is in our matching process when we're putting couples together. We've found over and over again that the more people's values match up the more likely they are to really have a connection. Many of our couples who were very similar in their strongest values areas are happily married or have been together for several years. In fact, we can't think of any cases where the relationship lasted when the two individuals didn't have clear correlations on values.

While we're not including our assessment in this book, you can go to www.lawsofthejungledating.com to take the assessment and find out how you rank on various traits. Ideally you'll be able to get your potential partner to do this too when the time comes. Even if you can't get a man to complete the assessment, you can at least know where you stand in the ranking on each trait and you can get a sense of which values are really the most important to you. You'll then be more aware of these characteristics in the men you're meeting and can better assess the possibilities for a long term, happy relationship. Here are the twelve characteristics, values and behaviors we believe are key indicators of the potential success of a relationship.

1. Introversion vs. Extroversion

We've already spoken about this. This is one area where opposites most often attract. It's interesting also to note that it's not infrequent that the two extremes will often come together, again in an effort to balance, and someone who is middle of the road on this trait will often be drawn to someone who is similarly in the middle of the road.

2. Connection

Here we're looking at the need to be connected to people, spend time with people versus having quiet alone time. The person that is high on connection gets his/her energy from being around people. This person doesn't have a big need for down time or quiet "alone" time. On the contrary, the person who is low on the need for connection can find that being around people on a constant basis drains their energy. They need quiet down time to themselves to re-energize. This is a trait where if opposites get together it can cause serious challenges in a relationship. The person that craves connection can easily feel hurt if they misinterpret the other partner's need for time away, time to themselves, as a reflection of that partner's level of love and commitment. Likewise, the partner who is low on the need for connection can feel smothered and suffocated by the other partner if they don't understand their partner's need for connectivity. This ultimately can wreak havoc on a relationship.

3. Flexibility

The trait of flexibility includes a variety of things including the person's natural level of spontaneity, their desire to, and enjoyment of trying new things; whether it's tasting new foods, exploring new places, or following new trends in design and fashion. The person that is high on flexibility often doesn't have to have every detail of a vacation itinerary planned out. The person who is low on flexibility often enjoys the planning process almost as much as the actual trip. They would also feel uncomfortable if solid plans weren't in place, whereas the person who is high on flexibility might feel constrained by too many plans. The person who is high on flexibility doesn't necessarily need to have a place for everything, and everything in its place, whereas the opposite is likely true for the person who is low on flexibility. The person who is high on flexibility is not likely to be terribly punctual, while the person who is low on flexibility sees punctuality as a very important value. You can see how partners who have differing values around flexibility will run into conflicts in their day-to-day lives. An unorganized closet or kitchen cabinet could drive one partner crazy, while the other partner just doesn't see this as a priority.

4. Parenting

Even if you don't have children and have no intention of having children, an individual's ideas about parenting still play a huge role in any relationship. Of course if either or both partners already have children, or if you're planning on having children, you had better figure this one out as much as you can in advance. No human being is ever going to be perfect, and the nature of relationships is going to bring up conflicts, so it's always a question of understanding the source of those conflicts and managing them to the best of our abilities. With the issue of parenting there are two ends of the spectrum: spare the rod, spoil the child; and children are meant to be seen and not heard; or the opposite end, which is one where children need complete freedom of expression and action to explore and develop into full human beings. Even if your children are grown and out of the house, or you don't have children, you'll still run into values around parenting. It could be that you're out for dinner and there are two little children at the table next to yours who are being less than quiet. To one partner, this could be seen as an intrusion on their quiet evening out for dinner. They might feel that parents shouldn't bring their young children out to a restaurant if they can't be controlled. To the other partner, they could see kids at the table next to them as just being normal little kids who are cute and full of energy, and isn't it great that a family is spending time together. Two obviously very different views of the same setting. Don't think for a second that this can't cause tension in a relationship. Of course if they're your own kids, or even worse, your partner's kids but not yours, the potential for conflict just multiplied tenfold. We suggest you check out where you are on our parenting scale.

5. Optimism

The question is do you have an optimistic, positive, upbeat, idealistic attitude and approach to life? Have you ever been accused of looking at life through rose-colored glasses? Or do you feel you're more realistic, pragmatic, cautious, sometimes skeptical, and maybe even a worrier, or negative in your approach to life? These differing viewpoints can be diametrically opposed to one another. They can have an impact on almost everything we do and say. They literally change the ways in which we live life. The person who's high on optimism can drive the person who's low on optimism almost insane with their Pollyanna approach to life. The person who's low on optimism constantly feels that their partner isn't being realistic; perhaps they even feel that they're being silly and childish by not taking into account the possible negative impacts a situation could have on their life. Meanwhile, the optimist could feel that their partner, who is low on optimism, is always dragging things down and not fully experiencing the joys of life because of their attitudes. They might also feel they're not being respected by their partner because of their partner's unwillingness to see the good in situations and the bright side of things. Again, if there are huge discrepancies in the two partners on this characteristic, there could be serious storms brewing.

6. Action Orientation

How active are you? This is not just physical activity in terms of sports and exercise, although this is certainly a part of action orientation. But are you constantly on the go? Do you find sitting and just watching TV or reading a book relaxing, or challenging? Do you need to be doing something while the TV is on? Do you find restful time is important for you to recharge? When you're on vacation do you prefer to lie on the beach with a book, or be constantly on the go, or a combination of both? We don't have to be clones of one another on this front, but if two partners are different, there needs to be some good understanding of one another so that both parties are comfortable when one is vegging out while the other is out and about. As with all differences in relationships, the more understanding there is around the other partner's needs, the more each can adjust to the other.

7. Care-Giving

Some people would think of this attribute as the mothering, or maternal instinct. Although this is by no means a characteristic that is exclusive to females; nor is it something that all females naturally possess. Care-giving really has to do with a person's natural tendencies and desires to nurture and care for someone. The idea is to understand how much you are drawn to tending to people and things in need of help. For example, do you find true fulfillment in nursing a sick child, or puppy, or is this something you see more as a necessity that you do because it's your responsibility or duty? Given a choice, would you prefer to have good qualified professionals care for an aging parent, or would you feel much better doing this yourself? Is there nothing you love more than holding and cuddling a newborn baby, or do you really prefer children that are a bit older who you can actually relate to? Do you love animals and feel you couldn't be without them in your life, or do you feel that some people are over the top in the place they give their pets in their lives? Differences on these values will have an impact on any relationship. They go to the core of how we relate to our friends and family members, and can't be overlooked.

8. Arts and Beauty

Are you passionate about the arts? Are you moved by a beautiful symphony, a romantic dance, a painter's masterpiece, or a stunning sunset? Do you find color and design to be an important part of your surroundings? Is the grandeur of nature something that you're constantly in awe of? Do you love photography and enjoy playing with light and texture? There are many different ways in which an individual can appreciate and express their sense of beauty and art. To some people this is highly important, while to others this sensitivity would barely create a blip on their radar screen. The more we have in common on these areas, the easier it is to build relationships with roots that can keep growing.

9. Intellectualism

If you are an avid reader, especially of non-fiction, you find history interesting, you love exploring ideas, engaging in a heady debate, challenging political ideals, and you highly value education and learning and being highly attuned to current affairs and world events, you're probably more of an intellectual than the population at large. Having a partner who shares your values and can hold their own in an intellectually stimulating conversation is probably very important to you. To the person who is considerably lower on intellectualism, this person might view the world more in terms of people and feelings rather than ideas and policies. Partners at opposite ends of the spectrum on intellectualism might have a difficult time relating to one another in the long run. They might each find the other rather boring and out of touch. The partner high on intellectualism might feel that the other partner doesn't know what's going on in the outside world, they're rather insular, and they don't grasp the issues affecting the world. In turn, the partner low on intellectualism could very well see the intellectual as out of touch with the day-to-day reality of truly connecting with people at the deepest level. Perhaps they see their partner as living in an ivory tower of ideals that are merely theoretical. Here are the makings for possible contempt on both sides if not understood in a relationship.

10. Expressiveness

The expressive has a need to be communicating, usually on many different levels and in different ways. The partner high on expressiveness is usually very verbal and is comfortable talking about his or her feelings and emotions. They can be highly emotional, easy to laugh out loud, easier to cry, and easier to show joy and happiness or anger and frustration. Another way an expressive might communicate is through physical touch. They might be quite tactile, cuddly, and higher on the need for physical affection. Expressives are not usually very private people, and they are generally not reserved about personal issues. The person who is lower on expressiveness doesn't feel comfortable showing their emotions in public. They would generally agree that the display of feelings should be held in check. Therefore they might be less tactile, and lower on the need for physical affection. If two opposite partners don't understand one another on this front there are lots of opportunities for lack of communication and hurt feelings.

11. Money Matters

The saver vs. the spender. As we all know, the challenge around money is one of the most common causes of stress in a relationship. It's not quite as simple as whether one partner is a saver and the other is a spender. It has to do with attitudes about money. Each person has a different level of risk tolerance. Each person has a different idea of what's important to spend money on, what's considered a luxury and what's considered a necessity. Some people believe money and what it can buy is important, other people don't place much importance on money. It can be something as simple as whether you'll spend money on parking your car for convenience versus parking for free, but having to walk three or four blocks. Whatever your views and attitudes are about money, it's imperative that you know where your prospective partner stands on this subject, and you feel you can live with their ideas on the subject. There's barely a day that goes by when we don't spend money, so values around money are bound to impact your relationship on a day-to-day basis.

12. Sensuality

This goes right to the heart of intimacy in the relationship. Differences in values, and likes and dislikes around physical touch, sex and sensuality can cause conflict and hurt in relationships. If one partner has a significantly higher sex drive than another, that partner can misinterpret the other partner's lack of interest in sex as a lack of interest in them and their relationship. This could very easily cause the partner with the higher sex drive to feel quite hurt. They could feel that they aren't sexy or attractive enough to their partner. On the other hand, if the partner who is more conservative and less adventuresome in their sexual likes and desires feels that they're being pushed into doing things they aren't comfortable with, this will cause conflict and possibly distrust in the relationship. Beware: there's little hope for a lasting fulfilling relationship if partners aren't reasonably in sync on their values in this area.

Linda's Story

Linda met Bill and there was definitely some chemistry, enough on both sides that they both wanted to meet a second time. By the third or fourth date it was clear that they both wanted to take this further. It seemed like there was lots of chemistry and lots in common in terms of lifestyle and shared experiences. In no time Linda and Bill were crazy about one another. They were really thrilled they had met and saw tons of potential in their budding relationship. There was certainly tons of attraction and chemistry. Everything was going well.

As with every relationship there were a couple of little hiccups, but that was to be expected, wasn't it? After all these were two adults in their mid-forties. Each of them had been divorced. Everyone comes to the table with some history, or "baggage." Linda and Bill were very good about discussing their challenges. They were both good at communicating, and they both wanted this to work. In fact, they "worked" at their relationship. And they "worked" at it, and they "worked" at it. After about four months of "working" at the relationship, Linda began to feel that maybe this really wasn't the right fit after all. Should a new budding relationship be this much "work"?

Finally, after another four months of "work," and several "breathers" in the relationship, Linda realized that although she and Bill really cared deeply about one another, respected one another, and were attracted to one another, it just wasn't right. They were too different. She looked at the characteristics and values in our Masterful Matchmaker Assessment and began to understand that a lasting relationship would never work for Bill and her. Linda was an extrovert and Bill was an introvert. That's fine, they could deal with that. However, Linda was very high on the need for connection and Bill was extremely low on this. Every second or third weekend Bill needed some quiet down time to himself. Linda felt extremely hurt every time this happened. He couldn't possibly love her as much as she loved him if he didn't want to be with her. Bill on the other hand felt Linda didn't respect him and his values because she was never on time for anything. Why did she always have to be five to ten minutes late? Couldn't she plan better so she didn't keep him waiting? Linda was too high on flexibility for Bill's lifestyle. She couldn't understand why he would get so upset if she was ten minutes late to meet him on a Saturday if they were just going for a walk. Linda was very much an optimist, and lived her life in a carefree and unworried way. Bill tended to be quite skeptical about things and tended to worry quite a bit. Linda felt like she was constantly trying to pull Bill up, and Bill felt like he was trying to bring Linda back down to earth. On money matters Linda and Bill probably couldn't have been more different. Bill kept an itemized daily log of every penny he spent. Saving money was like a sport to Bill. Bill thought he could really help Linda get her financial life together. Linda didn't worry about money. She enjoyed spending it freely, and there was always enough. Maybe just enough, but after all, you can't take it with you.

. . . .

You see, no matter how much Linda and Bill truly cared for each other, their values on some really critical issues were just too different. They were at opposite ends of the spectrum on too many things. No matter how hard they "worked" at their relationship, they weren't about to change each other on all of these fronts. It's just not possible.

If after dating someone for three to six months you find yourself dithering, feeling uncertain about the relationship, over-analyzing the relationship, or you find that the relationship is on and off, let it go. Don't settle for something that just doesn't fit. It's not right. If you have to "work" at a relationship at this stage it's just not the right one. This is where we strongly encourage you to listen to your heart. Linda will tell us today that in her heart she knew that her relationship with Bill wasn't going to work, but there was so much chemistry there that she kept trying.

✌ LAW OF THE JUNGLE ✌

After you've been dating someone for three to six months don't think, "blink"! You'll know when you've found Mr. Right. Go with your heart, with your gut instinct.

Go back to basics, the way things used to be when we were in our twenties. To find your perfect partner, first you have to think, don't blink. After some time of dating and getting to know him, blink, don't think!

Now that you know what you have to do to find your perfect partner, your Prince Charming, go out there and get him. Once you've found him, hang on to him for dear life. He's precious. Be sure to let him know it!

We hope you've enjoyed reading this book and found the stories and information in it interesting, eye-opening, practical, and helpful. We know that no matter how fantastic a book is, it can never change a person's life. It's only the *actions* a person takes as the result of new thoughts, ideas, and feelings from that book, that change a person's life. In order to change thought patterns we need a combination of high impact, high frequency and ongoing support. We need to practice new actions. We need to create and imbed new habits into our lives. None of this happens overnight because of reading one new book.

My mission is "to inspire, motivate and teach, thereby empowering people to discover, build, and grow living love in successful relationships." It's because of my sincere desire to help others experience wonderful loving relationships that we've developed a variety of programs to help keep your momentum going, and help you form and imbed new thought patterns, which will lead to new actions, which will lead to new *results*!

Check out our website

www.LawsOfTheJungleDating.com
or call 416-233-9541

for more information on any of the following programs.

RELATIONSHIP
MASTERY
PROGRAMS

Laws of the Jungle Dating 2 ½ Day Intensive Seminar

In this life altering, practical and immediately useable seminar you'll learn the laws of survival and ultimate success in the dating jungle that will really take you to the next level of change in your life beyond this book. In this highly experiential program you will learn the difference between the most successful daters that find love and fulfillment, and unsuccessful daters that experience struggle and despair. The information and principles in this session will lead you out of the jungle, transform your life and guarantee your success in finding the relationship of your dreams.

90-Day Relationship Attraction Conditioning Program – Workbook and Coaching

This program will support you in creating new thought patterns to help you attract your ideal mate.

90-Day Relationship Attraction Conditioning Workbook

In order for any of us to reprogram our thinking, it's been shown that we need to create new habits. Research shows that having a daily routine for a period of at least 90 days is the most effective way to really create new patterns in our thinking. This workbook gives you simple, quick, daily exercises to revise your "Relationship Attraction Imprint" and dramatically increase your ability to attract your perfect partner.

90-Day Relationship Attraction Conditioning Coaching

This one-on-one, highly specialized, unique coaching program is designed to ensure your success! None of us can do it alone. Even the best athletes in the world use coaches. Our proprietary system supports you in learning the secrets to attracting a great man or woman and a wonderful relationship, versus not attracting anyone, or attracting the wrong type of person. You'll be amazed at your results from this program!

Relationship Mastery Guided Imagery CD's

In this 3-CD set you'll be guided through an enlightening process to help you on the journey of finding your ideal mate. In these powerful sessions you will learn to create your reality from a place of conscious awareness, so that you become the guiding force in your life to attract the relationship that your heart truly desires. Let go of struggle and self-doubt to embrace love, light-hearted-ness, joy and faith in preparation for a wonderful new relationship with yourself and a partner.

This guided imagery set includes

- ∞ Preparing Yourself For Your Next Relationship
- ∞ Loving Yourself Completely
- ∞ Attracting Your Ideal Mate

Masterful MatchMaker Assessments

Self-knowledge and learning from these assessments help you build on a solid foundation to create more lasting love and happiness in your life. The surveys provide you with discernment tools to understand your relationship style and the personality traits and values that strongly influence your compatibility with a partner and increase your ability to have sustainable fulfillment and joy in your relationship. In short, they help you identify just who is Mr. or Ms. Right.

WITH GRATITUDE

As women in North America today we represent the largest and most influential buying market segment in the world. The "purse power" of women is truly astounding. And frankly, we have so much to be grateful for. Millions and millions of women and children around the world are living in dire situations and are in desperate need.

In celebration of the "purse power" of women, and as one small way to express gratitude for all of the good in our lives, and for the blessings received from the writing and sharing of this book, a percentage of the proceeds from the sale of each copy will be donated to the eWomen Network Foundation, a non-profit 501(c)(3) organization.

About the eWomen Network Foundation

The eWomen Network Foundation is dedicated to supporting the financial and emotional health of women and children. Funds raised are used to provide grants to small non-profit organizations across North America serving the needs of women and young girls. In addition, the Foundation supports the next generation of philanthropically inclined young professional women through its "Emerging Leader" program. The Foundation puts the eWomen Network philosophy "It takes teamwork to make the dream work" into action, and extends a helping hand to those who need it most. I invite you to join this crusade to "lift as we climb."

For more information about the programs of the Foundation go to www.ewomennetwork.com/foundation.html

If you'd like to make an additional donation to the Foundation please go to www.lawsofthejungledating.com and click on "The Purse Power of Women."

Thank you for your part in making this all possible, and helping less fortunate women and children.

Gloria

About the Authors

Gloria MacDonald

Gloria MacDonald is a Matchmaker, and the founder and CEO of Perfect Partners®, The Personal Relationship Executive Search Firm, a dating service for 40+ professionals. She started Perfect Partners because of her own personal experience finding herself single again in her mid-40's after 17 ½ years of marriage. Gloria found that the world of finding single, eligible men and dating was significantly different at this stage of life. Since 2003 she has worked with hundreds of single men and women to help them through the seeming jungle of dating.

Gloria believes the desire for love and companionship is basic to our nature and fundamental to our well being. She believes that the "**perfect partner**" is out there for anyone who has a sincere desire to find him or her. She's committed to helping people find that special match to share their laughter, joy, adventure and special moments with.

www.perfectpartners.ca

Thelma Beam

Thelma Beam has been a psychotherapist in private practice for 8 years. She specializes in helping men and women with relationship issues, individually and in couples counseling. Originally trained in psychoanalytic psychology, Thelma is also a certified hypnotherapist, a board certified regression therapist, and an NLP practitioner. She is a member of the International Board For Regression Therapy; The National Guild of Hypnotists; the American Association of Professional Hypnotherapists; and The National Federation of Neurolinguistic Psychology.

Before becoming a psychotherapist, Thelma worked for many years as a marketing research consultant. Currently, she is the principal of Mind Meld Consulting Inc., a marketing think tank which develops psychoanalytic models of consumer behavior.

www.MindMeldConsulting.com

Printed in the United States
115908LV00009B/13/A